SPECIAL RECOGNITION

Since I began teaching professionally in 1993, I have had the privilege of training 26 individuals to the rank of black belt in my system of combatives. Although the name was eventually changed to Roku Jutsu, the essence and guiding principles of the system have remained constant throughout the years. Through their dedication, hard work, and tenacity each of these students found a way to break through the wall of adversity. Toeing the line and paying the price: These are the warriors who earned the esteemed rank of black belt—and the expert power that comes with it.

Strength & Honor,
Chris Harris / Founder
Roku Jutsu Combatives

ROKU JUTSU BLACK BELTS

Armin Kashkooly	Jim Bussey
Blain Lancaster	Kristof Csaky
Brandon Foster	Marcoe Jackson
Bryce Lancaster	Mike Bentley
Chad Bentley	Randy Lancaster
Chris Bentley	Sean Henchey
Chris Clee	Shane Villars
Dan Matise	Shelbi Parker
David Busby	Stanton Harris
Dean Belvis	Travis Bentley
Dick Dandalides	Victor Andrade
Floyd Powell	William Clee
Jamie Colwell	William May

TABLE OF CONTENTS

FOREWORD

For more than two decades I have watched my husband, Chris, "go thru." From the first time I heard him speak on a stage before thousands to the times I witnessed him endure the wastelands or the belly of the beast, he has always managed to overcome whatever life throws his way. Chris' life reads like a story inspired by Joseph Campbell's *The Hero with a Thousand Faces*. At times, he almost sounds like a fictional, iconic archetype embodying the four masculine psychologies of the king, the warrior, the magician, and the lover. If I had not personally witnessed many of these stories, I might not believe it was the same man in all of them. Countless times I have told him, "If we made a movie out of your life, people would think it was fiction."

In 1996, before we exchanged vows, Chris told me he wanted me to see his past so I could decide if I wanted to be a part of his future. On a cold winter day in Ohio, he drove me from one memory to the next, stretching from the rural town where he graduated high school to the government projects where he last lived with his mother and two sisters. In each place we visited, he willingly opened old wounds and shared their hidden stories, offering me an unedited glimpse into his past.

At one point during this obscure odyssey, I was convinced he was trying to talk me out of being in love with him. He drove me to a remote farmhouse at the end of a long dirt driveway. It was an old gray house, worn and dying. Looking uncomfortably around me as he vividly described the foster family that boarded him there, I thought I was on the set of a horror movie. I say "family" loosely. He pointed up to the small circular window of the attic, indicating that was where his room was, while describing the old, mildewed twin mattress that had been his bed. He then explained, in great detail, the abuse and neglect he endured there as a child.

I buried my face in my hands and wept. I cried: "No more! I can't take anymore!" Chris stopped and gently laid his hand on my arm. I tried to compose myself enough to look at him. Here was this man I had known for only a short while, showing me the darkest parts of his childhood and it didn't seem to faze him—at all! I asked him how he could talk about these things with such ease? I didn't understand why he wasn't having an emotional reaction to seeing the farmhouse again or recounting these traumatic stories. With calmness in his voice, he looked me in the eyes and said: "Oh, I forgave them. I forgave all of them."

I was stunned by the inner strength of the man before me. I was stunned by how free he was, and I was stunned by the unlimited potential I saw in him. It was on that cold January day, surrounded by the ashes from the fires that forged him, that I fell deeply in love with his indomitable spirit. He was my match.

Since then, I have watched Chris metaphorically slay many dragons, rise from the gravel, spit out his blood and teeth—but still rise. I have seen him at the top of the mountain and in the depths of the valley. We have shared the worst of times and toasted the best. And through it all, this I can say: He is authentic, he is altruistic, he is brilliant, and he is a warrior.

In this book, the short stories shared by Chris represent genuine watershed moments, triumphs obtained through grit, and lessons learned the hard way. He admits his humanity, exposes his failures, and shares his victories—and all with the purpose of helping you break through the barriers that stand between you, your expert power, and the life you want most.

—Corrie A. Harris, M.A.
Wife since 1996, mother of our two children, and biggest fan.

As a bonus, many of the stories shared in this book have correlating photos that can be viewed in the gallery section of www.igothru.com.

INTRODUCTION

My purpose for writing this book can be summed up in one sentence: "The success that I want for myself, I want for everyone." Overcoming a tumultuous childhood and my firsthand experiences as a master combatives instructor have given me valuable insights into the significant impact of expert power. I am confident that when these principles are adopted and applied, they can advance your life significantly.

Just because the shortest distance between two points is a straight line, doesn't mean a straight line is the easiest journey. Life teaches us that the easiest journey is the one that has the fewest obstacles along the way. Metaphorically, these obstacles represent adversity and struggle. But it's the adversity that we experience throughout our lives that leads us to our greatest growth, development, and fulfillment. If we can muster the courage and persistence to "go thru" these obstacles, instead of going over, under, or around them, we will find our unique expert power on the other side.

For the premise of this book, expert power is defined as: *A unique genius that can only be earned by going thru the wall of adversity, and once earned, can never be taken away.*

Expert power isn't necessarily talent—one can be born with talent. It's not skill or training, although experts pursue both. It's the indomitable spirit that won't be kept down. It's the man in the arena who keeps rising, over and over. It's the grit and passion and persistence that defies unrelenting resistance and overwhelming odds. It's the will to go thru and get to the other side, despite the cost. The challenges you overcome become your expert power, your expert power becomes your story, and the next chapter of your story begins today!

—Chris Harris

1: EXPERTS GO THRU

For the premise of this book, expert power is defined as: A unique genius that can only be earned by going thru the wall of adversity, and once earned, can never be taken away.

Have you ever been faced with something difficult? Something challenging? Something that made you want to turn around and run the other way? I most certainly have. In fact, I've hit the proverbial brick wall on countless occasions throughout my life—truly! Sometimes due to unfortunate circumstances that were no fault of my own and other times due to accidents, mistakes, or downright poor choices. Regardless of the reason, the outcome was always the same—the accrual of knowledge based on the firsthand experience. But knowledge isn't power—as the saying would have us believe. It's "applied" knowledge that's power!

When faced with real adversity we have several options: We can face it head on, ignore it, look for shortcuts around it, or avoid it altogether. I believe that the best option is to go directly through it—without looking back! Going over, under, or around life's difficulties is certainly an effective strategy for minimizing pain and discomfort, but when we take one of these routes, we surrender our opportunity to gain authentic expert power as it relates to that experience. Having tried all of these options during my lifetime, I can honestly say that earning a new expert power is almost always the harder choice and leaves the thickest scars—but possessing it can pay a lifetime of invaluable dividends. The bottom line: Going through the hard stuff earns us firsthand experience that has the potential to become true power—but only if certain criteria are met.

To extract the really valuable stuff you have to separate the gold from the dross, which can only be accomplished by maintaining a positive attitude—long after the event is over.

Enduring difficulties and then feeling sorry for yourself, blaming others, or becoming embittered doesn't profit you anything—at least nothing worth mentioning. In fact, it hinders your personal growth and development and sets you back—possibly way back. If you want the good stuff, you need to load up the invaluable wisdom that was gained, lock it away in the vault, and send everything else to the junkyard. By salvaging the valuable stuff and reframing it into a positive, you meet the criteria for earning genuine expert power!

There will be countless friends and acquaintances who have known me for years who, after reading this book, will be surprised to hear some of the challenges I've faced in the past—especially those from my childhood. This is a fact that I'm proud of, and it's most certainly the point that I'm trying to make. I wholeheartedly believe in the importance of sharing the trials and tribulations from our life's journey with others, especially the lessons learned along the way—but only if it inspires and encourages others. I view adversity, struggle, and hardship as life's greatest teachers—it's the kind of training that makes champions for life. So, go through the wall that stands before you head on, keep a positive attitude every step of the way, and earn your authentic expert power. And if you fall during the process, that's OK too, just do your best to fall forward—because experts go thru!

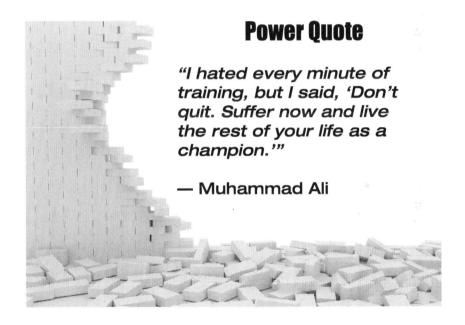

Power Quote

"I hated every minute of training, but I said, 'Don't quit. Suffer now and live the rest of your life as a champion.'"

— Muhammad Ali

2: EXPERTS WORK WITH WHAT THEY HAVE

Living in the projects in 1977 in Dayton, Ohio, taught me many valuable lessons that I will never forget. Having just turned 10 years old, I was one of the only Caucasian kids living in this Section 8 government housing at the time and was definitely the minority. I was chased on foot nearly every time I was seen stepping outside of our small corner unit. The two biggest problems with this scenario were: I was a slow runner, and I didn't know how to fight. It didn't take long for me to learn the importance of lying in a fetal position with my arms covering my head and face until the group of bullies disbanded.

One day, a devout Christian man from the local church showed up in my neighborhood, and it changed my life forever, but not in the way most would think. He was a black belt in karate and wanted to volunteer his time by providing a free service to our community. Keenly aware that most of the boys living there were not being raised by fathers, he wanted to teach us self-discipline and self-respect through the martial arts, and offer himself as the positive male role model we so desperately needed.

Classes were conducted in the recreation center near the entrance of our community. It was a square one-story building with lots of large windows along each wall. At one point, it had housed bumper pool and Ping-Pong tables, but that was short-lived. I was so excited about the first class that I couldn't sleep the night before. I would be giving up my highly coveted Saturday morning cartoons to attend but didn't care—I was about to learn karate! When I walked into the rec center, the neighborhood bullies began yelling at me to get out, pushing me toward the door, and threatening to hurt me, if I didn't leave immediately. To my surprise, the instructor acquiesced to their abrupt protest and politely asked me to leave, making some spiritual comment about having to consider the greater good.

It was the dead of winter, it was freezing, and a light flurry of snow was in the air. I did not own a coat or socks, but I did have on my Toughskins jeans, long-sleeve paisley silk shirt, and my Kmart-brand gym shoes, so I was good to go and ready to learn! I stood outside the plate glass window and mimicked every move, during every class, without exception. And I practiced diligently throughout the week. I was eager, I was committed, and I wasn't about to let a window or freezing temperatures stop me! Week after week, lesson after lesson, the instructor (and the class) watched my skills improve with every technique I performed. It soon became obvious that I had a natural gift for the martial arts, and this talent coupled with my unbridled dedication caused me to evolve quickly.

My commitment to work with what I had—despite the conditions and obstacles—eventually caused the instructor to invite me back inside. I had obviously earned some respect from the bullies too, because they were no longer asking me to leave. Standing in the back of the room, I excelled even quicker, and eventually I found myself standing in the front, next to the instructor, assisting as he led the class. It was the first time in my life I was truly passionate about something, and I wanted more.

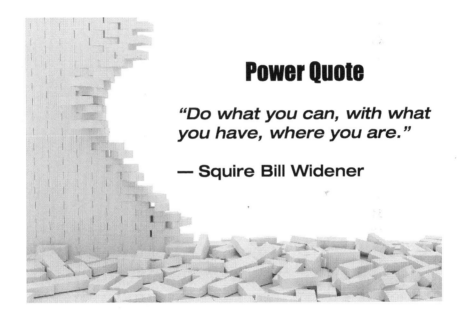

Power Quote

"Do what you can, with what you have, where you are."

— Squire Bill Widener

3: EXPERTS CONFRONT THEIR FEARS

I used to teach hand-to-hand combat to civilians in a 1,200-square-foot metal-sided warehouse with a 14-by-14-foot roll-up door. Nestled between several small automotive shops, it didn't have AC to help during the Texas summer or heat for the winter. This meant we relied on fans and space heaters to make things bearable, not to mention good old-fashioned grit. On occasion, we would have 25 students packed in this hot metal box on a Saturday morning, and as uncomfortable as it was, nobody ever complained. Our school mascot was a very personable and highly intelligent black dog named Sparqi, who loved to walk around and say hi to everyone, whenever it suited him. Sometimes, he even wore a school T-shirt—just because he could.

The floors were bare concrete; the only exception was a 12-by-12-foot matted area that was framed with two-by-fours and mounted in the center of the room. Adhered to this red mat was a 12-inch-long piece of black tape that represented the essence of everything we taught. This simple piece of tape was referred to as THE FEAR LINE. When you stepped up to it, and put your toes on it, you were indicating to any black belt in the room that you were ready to be attacked, with anything they could muster, at any time. With your feet together and your hands by your side, you purposely made yourself vulnerable and confronted your fear of being hit, being hurt, and being embarrassed.

For new students, stepping up to the fear line was a major ordeal and took a great amount of courage. But, over time, as their experience and skill set improved, so did their confidence. And as their confidence improved, so did their performance. When a new student was told to toe the line, they did so with fear and trembling, but they still did it—they just did it afraid. Courage at its finest!

19

Writing this book has required me to step up to the line and confront my fears, and with every chapter a new dose of anxiety is unleashed. What if nobody reads or listens to this book after I've invested all this time and effort? What if nobody likes the book and it gets criticized by a handful of anonymous haters on social media? What if the audience judges me? Or worse yet, rejects me? These are the thoughts I deal with each and every time I sit down at my computer to write. So why do I press through, exposing my humanity and vulnerability? My answer is simple: I choose to focus on a better narrative. What if someone is inspired to change, moved to forgive, or challenged to overcome? If only one person is encouraged to take steps to advance their life, isn't that enough, doesn't that make it all worth my while? Can one person who achieves triumph overcome the voices of a thousand naysayers? My answer is an emphatic, yes! As I go thru, I will invite "fear the counselor" to sit on my shoulder and whisper wisdom in my ear. And, I will reject "fear the jailer," who tries to stand in my way and shouts lies to my face. Because this book has the potential to help just one, I am resolute to finish it—even if I have to do it afraid.

Power Quote

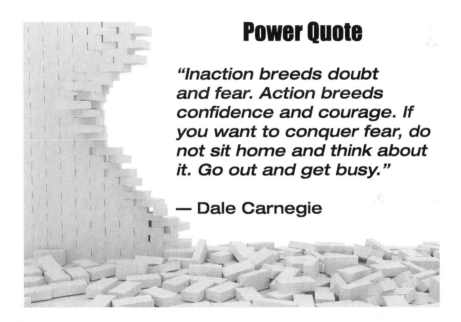

"Inaction breeds doubt and fear. Action breeds confidence and courage. If you want to conquer fear, do not sit home and think about it. Go out and get busy."

— Dale Carnegie

4: EXPERTS EARN TRUST

Asking a trained soldier or law enforcement officer to hit you in the face as hard and as fast as they can, while surrounded by their peers, may not seem like a good idea to most people. In fact, it may seem like pure stupidity. But that's exactly what I did, countless times, over the years. When I arrived at a facility to provide hand-to-hand combat training, the attendees were sometimes less than receptive to me being there. Perhaps they had never heard of me, weren't told I was coming, or didn't believe I possessed the necessary skill set to be giving instructions on the topic at hand. Whatever their reasons, I had to begin the process of establishing trust immediately, or I might be shown the door and would not be invited back.

A pride of lions is made up of adult males and females, as well as their cubs. A coalition of lions, however, is made up of a small group of adult males, who may be responsible for protecting one or more prides within a given territory. Anytime I showed up to teach a group for the first time, I knew I was being evaluated by their internal coalition. I knew that my skill set had to be verified by these select few before trust would be given by the group as a whole. And, I knew that trust had to be earned before knowledge could be transferred. Lenders verify with credit checks, employers verify with background checks, and warriors verify with ability checks. I once saw a sign hanging above the entrance of a caged octagon fighting ring that read: "In here, you can't hide what you don't know." By openly inviting a physical attack from a member of the coalition at the beginning of a new class, I was asking to be verified by exposing what I knew (or didn't know) to the collective body—and at great risk.

The first attack would usually come halfheartedly and at a medium speed—and I would evade and counter with very little effort, entangling the attacker in an uncomfortable control and restraint technique at the end. It was always the second attempt that was loaded with seriousness and weighted with the real threat of danger. And yet again, the same as the first time, I would successfully evade and counter while matching the attacker's speed and intensity tit for tat, followed by a lock or a hold. After two unsuccessful attempts at putting hands on me, one halfhearted and one all out, I would earn the respect required to take control of the class and could finally get down to business.

In all my years of teaching combatives professionally, not once was I successfully hit by a student while performing this trust-building exercise. I had obtained this authentic expert power on the streets and in the arena by the hardest means possible, and I never hesitated to validate my qualifications when a job was on the line. When you possess real expert power, you should never squawk or balk at the request to prove that your words and actions are in alignment. The fact that someone is asking shows that they want to trust you, and your willingness and openness to mitigate their concerns goes a long way toward proving that you are the real deal. Remember, just because someone offers you their trust doesn't mean you don't have to prove your salt—so stand tall, maintain eye contact, and always be prepared to verify.

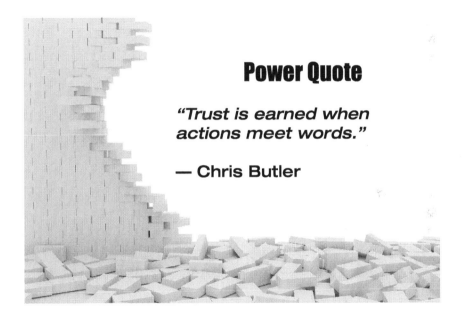

Power Quote

"Trust is earned when actions meet words."

— Chris Butler

5: EXPERTS FOLLOW THEIR INSTINCTS

At 27 years old I was single with no kids and had mixed feelings about the thought of getting married. During my childhood, I had witnessed a string of loveless marriages that were laced with infidelity and varying types of abuse. As a young adult, I was keenly aware of the staggering divorce rate and was already seeing my friends from high school live out these statistics. As to becoming a father, I was concerned whether I was up for that task as well, given my traumatic experiences as a child. Nonetheless, I was open to the idea of having a family one day but also wondered if it would be better if I remained single.

On December 15, 1995, I called the church I was attending and asked for Debbie, who was responsible for coordinating the volunteer schedule for the children's ministry. I was letting her know that I would no longer be able to serve as a volunteer on Sundays, since I would soon be moving to another city. I had negotiated a one-year law enforcement training contract in Houston, and my team and I needed to be there within 30 days to begin work. Debbie responded by saying: "That's too bad, because I really wanted to introduce you to my sister, Corrie. I think the two of you would really hit it off." With great interest, I encouraged her to set up a meeting between her sister and me, and we both agreed that if it was meant to be, it was meant to be.

Not wasting any time, the blind date was scheduled for that evening. I was to meet Corrie in the food court at the local mall, with Debbie there to make the formal introduction. As I approached the food court, I caught my first glance of Corrie from 50 yards away, and my heart nearly leapt out of my chest. Standing in front of her, I kept saying to myself, "Oh my goodness, she's the one." Noticing the obvious chemistry, Debbie introduced us with a grin on her face, then hung around for a few minutes of small talk until her sister gave her the stealthy nod of approval—signaling that she could take it from here.

Corrie and I left the mall and headed to a local restaurant where we enjoyed a fabulous meal with lots of meaningful conversation (even though I forgot my wallet). Recalling a word I learned from watching the movie *Bambi* as a child, I found myself undoubtedly "twitterpated" and could hardly hold myself together. In fact, by the end of dinner, with confidence and frankness, I looked her square in the eyes from across the table and told her that I was definitely going to marry her. Stunned by my boldness, she decided to take a chance on love at first sight and see where it took us.

Fifteen days later, on December 30, while on a Christmas light tour in a horse-drawn carriage, I got down on one knee with a ring in hand—and popped the question. With both of us moonstruck, she agreed to be my wife, and 10 weeks later we were married in a church in East Texas. And, due to an unexpected chain of events, my team and I didn't move to Houston after all. Because I trusted my heart and confronted my fears, my remarkable wife and I have been married for 24 years and counting, embracing life's challenges as they come. Isn't it amazing how quickly things can change for the better when we get out of our head and follow our instincts?

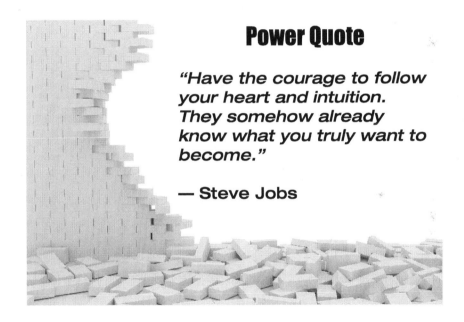

Power Quote

"Have the courage to follow your heart and intuition. They somehow already know what you truly want to become."

— Steve Jobs

6: EXPERTS TAKE THEIR POWER BACK

How many miles would you drive to offer your forgiveness to someone who had hurt you deeply but didn't care? For me, it was a thousand miles. Let me explain.

Shortly after moving from Texas to North Carolina, my wife and I were about to have our first child. The thought of being a parent terrified me, due to all the trauma and neglect I had experienced growing up—mainly from my mother. After weeks of turmoil, I knew it was time to confront this part of my past head on so that I could move forward with my future. In short, it was time to face my mom.

My wife and I loaded up the vehicle and drove over 500 miles from Raleigh to visit my mother, who was in a nursing home in Cincinnati. Having not seen my mother in several years, I nervously walked down the long, dingy hallway to her shared room, with my wife by my side and one significant sentence that I had to deliver.

I looked my 48-year-old mother square in the eyes as she sat in the manual wheelchair where she was permanently confined, due to years of selfish choices and epic heroin abuse. Then, I leaned down, hugged her neck, and offered her my unconditional forgiveness—for everything. This meant I forgave her for the abandonment, the abuse and neglect, for the 18 public schools and countless foster homes I had to endure, for being permanently separated from my sisters, for having to live on the streets while eating from dumpsters, and most of all, for seeing things that no child should ever have to see.

My mother's response to my heartfelt offering was simple. She backed up her wheelchair so she could scan me with a broader field of view while she tilted her head in disgust and spewed these words: "Why in the hell do I need your forgiveness?"

Standing there next to my wife, both of us stunned and speechless after this most unexpected response, I finally realized that the purpose of this 1,000-mile roundtrip journey was not to give something to my mother. Instead, it was to take something back, and that was my POWER. At that moment, I imagined removing the brown vial of bitter poison that I had been carrying in my heart for over 20 years and laying it on the small table in her windowless room while saying to myself: "I am leaving this poison here for you to do with as you wish, because I don't want it anymore. I am leaving here free from the pain of my past. I am leaving with nothing but forgiveness in my heart, and I am leaving with my power!"

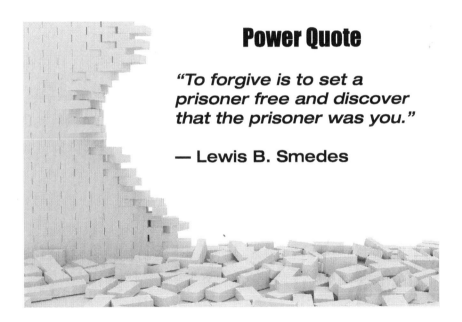

Power Quote

"To forgive is to set a prisoner free and discover that the prisoner was you."

— Lewis B. Smedes

7: EXPERTS RIDE THE BENCH

I loved high school! Dodge ball during gym class, the smell of the locker room, cafeteria food, '80s music—I loved it all. Bethel was a small school in the country, with the elementary, middle school, and high school all on the same campus. When I transferred to Bethel from a town just 15 minutes away, where I'd been living with foster parents, I made up my mind that I was going to stay until graduation—no matter what. Before arriving there, I had attended 18 public schools, due to jumping around between foster homes—as well as all the moving I did with my mother. Eighteen schools had been more than enough, and I was determined to make #19 my last, even if I had to fake it to make it.

It didn't take me long to learn that the key to getting plugged in was through sports. The only problem was, I sucked at sports! With only 84 kids in my graduating class, most of them had been attending Bethel since kindergarten and had been playing sports together since they were old enough to throw a ball. Even though I had no skills or experience, I knew I could make most teams, simply because the coaches always needed players. Baseball and football were my favorites; I ran track and cross-country for a few seasons, and I stayed as far away from a basketball as humanly possible. Considering the fact that I was a slow runner who struggled with catching, throwing, and hitting, I somehow seemed to manage.

Years earlier, while living in the projects, I came to recognize that I had a gift for the martial arts, but that would not help me at Bethel. And, it would be years before that gift would be fully developed. The good news was, there was an exceptional man who lived across the street from my high school who taught martial arts and helped me in ways I'll never forget. The bad news was, between school, sports, and work, finding time to make it to his classes was always a challenge.

35

I did my best to fit in with my classmates, but the truth was, like most teenagers, I was insecure. And, my insecurity typically manifested itself through jokes, sarcasm, and being cocky. Despite my shortcomings, I chose to keep my chin up and keep practicing—because it was never about the sport or the game. For the first time in my life, I was exposed to coaching, leadership, team conditioning, and most importantly—friends. This is why I played.

During all four years of high school, I tried to always be on a team. I practiced with the guys, suited up on game days, sat in the player's section during the pep rallies—and rode the bench during the games. On the one hand, it was embarrassing and humiliating, especially during those times that I sat through an entire game without ever stepping on the field. On the other hand, for the first time in my life, I felt like I was truly part of something great. I practiced hard, I cheered hard, and oftentimes, I took it hard. But now, looking back, I see things differently, more clearly. Not only did those countless hours of riding the pine build much-needed character, they taught me how to be a team player. And through it all, the thing I will remember the most is how the comradery and strong sense of belonging got me through high school. I'll take the bench over the bleachers any day.

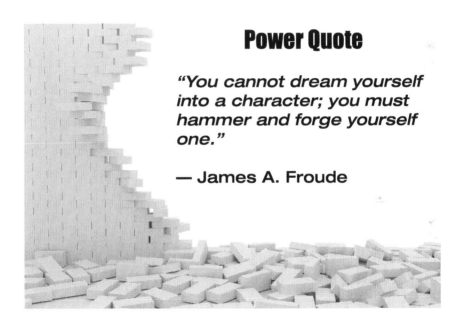

Power Quote

"You cannot dream yourself into a character; you must hammer and forge yourself one."

— James A. Froude

8: EXPERTS TAKE THE LEAP

In 1985 I looked like your typical high school senior from the Midwest. My go-to attire was a pair of Levi's, Nike gym shoes, a sweatshirt with the sleeves cut off, and a long-sleeved thermal undershirt underneath. On the passenger seat of my car, I had an old shoe box filled with cassette mix tapes of my favorite '80s music. I commonly recorded groups like Journey, Def Leppard, and Alabama all on the same cassette, which would become so worn that I would have to rewind them by hand and with the help of a #2 pencil. During football practice one of my teammates would take large speakers from his house (that he kept in his trunk) and set them on the roof of his '70s sedan. The sound was so loud that it was distorted, but we didn't care. In fact, we loved it!

Nonetheless, as fun and as cool as that was, I knew three things to be true: I had to leave Ohio immediately following graduation, I couldn't look back, and college wasn't for me (at least not yet). I had to distance myself from the pain of my childhood so I could view things objectively, from a safe distance. I needed a place where I could process the confusion in my own way and at my own pace. Even though I was 18 and legally an adult, I was still just a boy in many regards. I had to find my right of passage—take my very own walkabout. If I could find a place where I could enter as a boy and walk out a man, I was committed to do the work and ready to take the leap.

When I met with the Air Force recruiter, enlisting for four years of active duty was a fairly efficient process. Within the span of a few weeks I completed the paperwork, took some tests, passed my physical, swore an oath, and was given a date to report to basic training in Texas. I was anxious to get there and was literally counting down the days. I knew what would happen if I stayed in Ohio. If I didn't take this leap now, I would either stall from my fear, self-destruct from my anger, or settle for a life of poverty out of self-pity. For me, August 30, 1985, could not come soon enough!

Traveling from Dayton to Lackland Air Force Base in San Antonio made for a very long day. All I took with me were the clothes on my back, whatever would fit in my small gym bag, and a $20 bill. From the moment I stepped off the bus and onto the base, my highly trained drill sergeant was there to greet me with the intensity of a tsunami. Over the next few months, with his Smokey the Bear hat, his perfectly pressed uniform, and his highly polished boots, he shaped me and my squadron of 52 airmen like a master swordsmith forges a new blade. Never relenting, he pounded away—heating, bending, and hammering us, each and every day.

The next several years would prove to be the hardest yet most formidable years of my life. God bless the United States Military for giving me a solid place to land and for teaching me to be a responsible man with a strong work ethic. I will forever remain grateful.

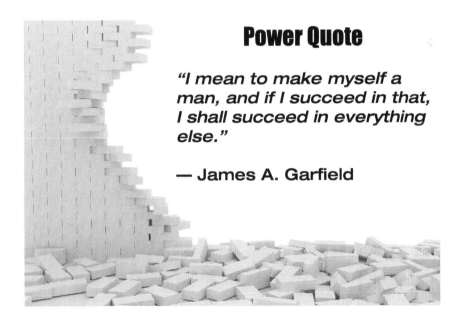

Power Quote

"I mean to make myself a man, and if I succeed in that, I shall succeed in everything else."

— James A. Garfield

9: EXPERTS CREATE THEIR DEATH GROUND

In Sun Tzu's book, *The Art of War*, he wrote of the benefit of intentionally creating a "death ground," which is something immovable that eliminates the possibility of escape. This could be a geographical feature, such as a river or a mountain, or intentionally setting the woods on fire. The reasoning is simple: We fight more fiercely when death is viscerally present.

In December 2006, with our son in second grade and our daughter in kindergarten, my wife and I strategically created our very own death ground by shutting down my successful business and selling everything we owned. The reason for this was to finance one larger-than-life decision, and that was to move our family of four from North Carolina to Nicaragua, so that we could assume the role of directors of an orphanage. We knew that we would have to stay at least two years in order to make an impact, so we created this death ground to prevent an early retreat.

Knowing there would be no promise of income or financial support for the next two years, we gathered the money we would need to sustain ourselves by selling our five-bedroom house, our furniture, both cars, our 34-foot RV, and my motorcycle. In short, other than the duffle bags we took with us, our only other possessions were the plastic bins filled with keepsakes and memorabilia that were locked away in a 10-by-10-foot storage unit, back in Raleigh. When the four of us boarded the airplane to Central America on Christmas Eve, we did so without a home base back in the States.

The orphanage, which we affectionately referred to as La Villa, was a 500-acre farm with 16 concrete buildings that were outfitted to house up to 100 children. It was located in a rural area, about 20 miles from the capital city of Managua, and owned by the church that we had attended back in the States.

We didn't speak Spanish, and we didn't know the culture, but we did know how to lead, how to manage, and how to care deeply, which we hoped would be enough. Fully aware of our strengths and shortcomings, my wife, Corrie, and I entered into this massive endeavor with one simple commitment to each other: to give it everything we had and to leave nothing on the table, which was exactly what we did.

Nicaragua is one of the poorest countries in the Western Hemisphere, second only to Haiti, with the average person earning the equivalent of one U.S. dollar per day. In addition to extreme poverty conditions, they were striving to overcome the aftereffects of dictatorship, civil war, and natural calamities. During our two-year stay, we addressed enormous challenges, such as standing between the children we cared for and their abusive family members, complying with prohibitive laws, providing aid to the neighboring villages, venemous snakes, food and water parasites, and a host of others.

Despite the difficulties, it was a beautiful chapter in our lives, and we wouldn't change a thing. And, most importantly, because we put ourselves on death ground and stayed the course, this journey will forever remain one of my family's most cherished memories, grand experiences, and greatest privileges.

Power Quote

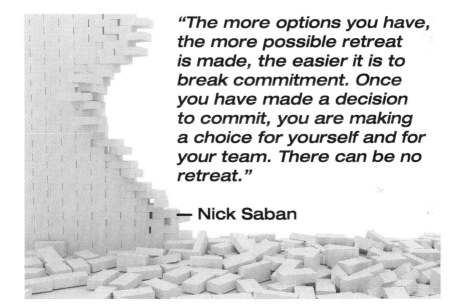

"The more options you have, the more possible retreat is made, the easier it is to break commitment. Once you have made a decision to commit, you are making a choice for yourself and for your team. There can be no retreat."

— Nick Saban

10: EXPERTS CHOOSE THEIR PERSPECTIVE

My two sisters and I were permanently separated from each other when I was 10 years old. The day the police drove my mother away in handcuffs was the same day that child protective services drove my sisters and me away, in separate cars. We were each a year or so apart, making them around 11 and 12 at the time—and making it a very emotional day. Over the next several years, the three of us would live in countless homes, all in the same city, but never under the same roof again.

By the time my sisters were 18, both of them were struggling with severe drug addictions and were entrenched in an all-out war with the demons that accompany that lifestyle. As adults, we would see each other briefly, every 10 years or so, but we would never again know each other as brother and sisters. I made it out, they didn't, and we would forever remain worlds apart.

Regarding my childhood, the one question that I've been asked the most during my adult life is: "How did you make it out, but your sisters didn't, even though you were raised under the same circumstances?" I must admit, I don't believe in my lifetime that I will ever fully know the answer to this question. However, I have found comfort in the words from Deuteronomy 29:29, which reads, in part: "The secret things belong to the Lord our God." Put simply, it alleviates the pressure of me feeling like I have to know the answer. From a spiritual perspective, I accredit every good thing in my life to God's amazing grace, and I try not to read into it much further than that.

My "non-spiritual" response to this question is somewhat different, as it points everything toward the fruit of perspective and attitude. As adults, both of my sisters would blame most (if not all) of their harsh circumstances on either their childhood or our mother. And, although we would only see each other a handful of times over the years, their stories never seemed to change—not even slightly. During my teenage years and as an adult, I have remained adamant about adopting and maintaining a perspective that was opposite that of my sisters'. A perspective free from blame and self-pity and an attitude of gratefulness.

Metal is annealed at temperatures ranging from 500 to 1,400 degrees Fahrenheit to improve its strength, hardness, toughness, and corrosion resistance. Annealing also improves a metal's ductility, which is its ability to be stretched into a thin wire without becoming weak or brittle. I choose to view my childhood as my time in the blazing furnace, when I was annealed into the man I am today. The heat and pressure from my upbringing have made me stronger, harder, and tougher. It was during my time as a boy on the streets of Dayton, Ohio, that I learned to survive without becoming brittle and to cultivate a heart that is free from corrosion. I will always view these formative years as one of my greatest blessings; they prepared me to succeed and, more importantly, to help others along the way. It is because of my childhood that I Go Thru!

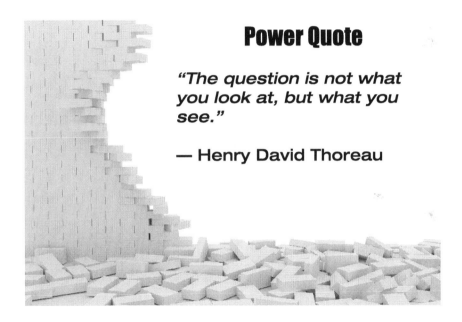

Power Quote

"The question is not what you look at, but what you see."

— Henry David Thoreau

11: EXPERTS ARE SELF-AWARE

Teaching combatives to non-civilians is a feast-or-famine business. To help mitigate the financial dry seasons associated with this fulfilling career, I decided to take a successful businessman up on his offer. In 2000 the president of Sirchie asked me to come work for his company. Founded in 1927, Sirchie is a global leader in forensic science and crime scene investigation products, and their world headquarters was only 30 minutes from my home in Raleigh. I would be working exclusively with law enforcement, military, and federal agencies, which was a natural fit to my existing customer base. I agreed to take the job under the condition that I would be an employee for one year—just long enough to learn the ropes. But after that, I would switch to an independent contractor, allowing me to work from home, control my schedule, and continue to build my combatives business.

During my six years as an independent contractor for Sirchie, one of my core responsibilities was to teach an eight-hour training certification course to agencies that purchased certain high-end forensic science technology that we manufactured. I trained and certified law enforcement, military, crime labs, FBI, CIA, and others. In all, I taught our certification course approximately 200 times to nearly 500 agencies. The most challenging part of my instructor responsibilities was continually being scrutinized by professionals who are known for giving extremely honest feedback. Their comments were delivered both verbally and via written evaluations—and were typically highly accurate. I will always remember this season of my life as the time I developed true self-awareness and achieved a new expert power.

Receiving honest feedback is an important component of improving one's self-awareness, but only if the recipient chooses to act on the information in a positive way. My first hurdle was learning how to process this steady stream of professional critiques without taking it personally. During my first year of teaching these classes, I wanted to stop passing out the written evaluations altogether, because I associated them with personal rejection. But I knew if I could improve in this area, the benefits would be far-reaching, so I swallowed my pride and took each opinion offered in stride. Eventually, I began to view critiques and criticism as road maps that contained detailed instructions on how to arrive at a better future. Once I finally made this mental shift, I welcomed all performance-related feedback.

First, I had to accept the fact that the expert power I had earned as a combatives instructor did not transfer to this group of investigators and scientists—at all. I would have to earn my stripes, one at a time. I began conducting self-audits by videoing my classes, which resulted in improvement of my nonverbal skills and the development of a more positive teaching style. Watching myself, I was embarrassed by how negative I was. I caught myself frequently using sarcasm and humor to mask my nervousness; this tactic would have to be discarded completely. I switched from "only telling my stories" to sharing inspiring customer stories, making it less about me and more about them. I began to pay attention to the facial expressions and body language of my audience, adjusting to their needs instead of being rigid and inflexible. I started placing more value on the students' time by always starting and ending on time—no more late starts. I had to really stretch myself to connect with students on a personal level—instead of a transactional one. I began to share my strengths and weaknesses equally, whenever appropriate. I learned how to manage my emotions when students were disruptive in class by responding instead of reacting. And when I made a mistake, I owned it immediately and moved on— reflecting and adjusting once the class was over. Lastly, I learned to read the social cues that I had always missed before and became a better listener. Over time, my heightened level of self-awareness translated to improved self-acceptance, which has made me a better teacher, husband, father, and friend.

Power Quote

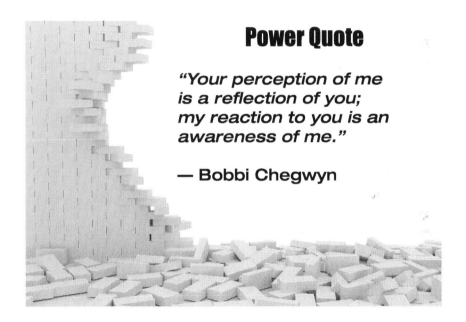

"Your perception of me is a reflection of you; my reaction to you is an awareness of me."

— Bobbi Chegwyn

12: EXPERTS PRIORITIZE

Do you ever get stressed out or overwhelmed with everything you've got to get done—too much to do with too little time? If so, I'd like to introduce you to a combatives principle called *primary and secondary* that can have a major impact on your life, if properly and consistently applied.

Imagine you're watching a blockbuster action movie and the hero is an *elite covert operative* who is walking through a poorly lit parking garage while heading toward his black-on-black SUV. Then, all of a sudden, he finds himself surrounded by five expert henchmen who were sent to do him great harm. In the blink of an eye he does a visual scan of the situation then begins the process of physically disseminating the group of bad guys, one by one, with nothing but his bare hands. Impressive, right? So how did he manage to do all of this while never losing his head and always remaining in control of the situation? Is this just Hollywood theatrics, or can someone really be taught to handle things this way?

As a master combatives instructor, one of my key responsibilities is to teach students how to remain calm and focused when faced with the appearance of overwhelming odds. To accomplish this, the student should never process more than two threats at a time. This means that, regardless of the number of attackers, the student must always keep the crisis manageable and not lose their cool. To carry this out, the student quickly determines which aggressor they consider to be the highest-level threat and flags them in their mind as the primary target. Simultaneously, in their peripheral, they are choosing the secondary target that will be confronted next. Once the primary has been neutralized, the secondary becomes the new primary, and the process repeats itself until all threats are eliminated. By following this system of threat reduction, a crisis gets segmented into smaller, more manageable pieces, resulting in less stress and fewer mistakes.

One thing that separates experts from novices is that experts are keenly aware of the importance of effectively managing and guarding their time, their mindset, and their stress. By incorporating these principles of "prioritize and reduce" into your daily routine, you are much less likely to feel surrounded by all that has to get done. To implement this, if you find yourself feeling overwhelmed, say out loud the two things that must be done first and engrave them on your mental calendar as your primary and secondary priorities. Then, give them your full and undivided attention. Nothing more, nothing less, nothing else. For this process to work, you must train your mind to stay on point, without drifting and without exception!

By intentionally directing your energy and efforts toward accomplishing just two things at a time, you will be exercising the signature principle behind the law of economy of motion. Remember, always complete the primary before bumping the secondary to the front of the line, then recruit your new secondary, and rinse and repeat. Once this is mastered, your efficiency and productivity will increase, your cortisol levels will decrease, and you will experience more peace in the process.

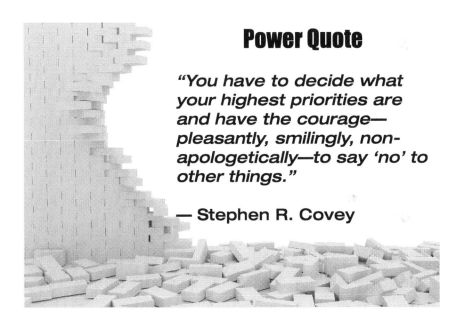

Power Quote

"You have to decide what your highest priorities are and have the courage— pleasantly, smilingly, non- apologetically—to say 'no' to other things."

— Stephen R. Covey

13: EXPERTS FALL FORWARD

In the game of basketball there are flagrant fouls, intentional fouls, and technical fouls. In the arena of life, there are accidents, mistakes, and poor choices—each is uniquely different. If, while driving on the interstate, you run someone off the road while trying to avoid hitting a deer, that's an accident. If you run them off the road because they were in your blind spot, that's a mistake. And, if you run them off the road because you were typing a text, that's a poor choice. If we are going to learn and grow from these types of life events, it's crucial that we label them correctly. Failing a written exam that you studied for versus failing a written exam that you refused to study for is not the same thing—not even close. When we call our poor choices "accidents or mistakes" we avoid taking full responsibility for our part in the matter—stunting our personal development. If we genuinely want to learn and grow from something we've done wrong, we first must own it—so the rest of the process can properly unfold.

When I'm training someone in close quarters combat, I teach them to boldly say "HIT" every time a technique or drill is done incorrectly, which represents acknowledgment, apology, and release. And, they must say it loud enough for everyone in the room to hear. The student is not permitted to give an excuse, and they're not allowed to dwell on the mistake with negative self-talk or body language. During the first few months of training, the practice of always saying "HIT" is challenging for most people, and it has to be constantly reinforced throughout each lesson. Oftentimes, I have to stop a student in the middle of a bad technique and ask, "What are you forgetting that's important?" For most, verbally admitting that they've made a mistake to the class and the instructor is difficult, especially since no additional commentary can follow their public declaration. However, after it's repeated enough times, the mandatory requirement of always having to say "HIT" disciplines the practitioner to instinctively do three things:

1) Acknowledge that they've done something wrong, without making excuses.

2) Take personal ownership of their part in the matter, without negative self-talk.

3) Forgive themselves, let it go, and continue forward—now smarter and wiser.

When we make huge mistakes or really bad decisions, whether deliberately or unintentionally, it is as if we have metaphorically fallen down, perhaps even face first—on the pavement. When this happens, we will likely experience guilt, regret, remorse, and possibly even shame. Dealing with these negative emotions is often part of the learning phase, as well as the recovery process. And, if these emotions must be consumed to aid us in our healing, it's important that we extract whatever medicinal value they can offer, then spit them out—before they become toxic. And remember, these four emotions can become addictive for some—so no refills.

Falling is part of life's journey, and it's the price we pay for putting ourselves out there while attempting to live a full and meaningful life. It's the speed and the direction that we rise—and the number of times that we get back up—that truly sets us apart. So, the next time you find yourself lying on the asphalt covered in your self-imposed rubble and grime, say "HIT," pack up the lesson, and move on down the road. And the next time you find yourself in a tight spot on the highway of life, remember this: Conviction will always offer you an exit, but condemnation never does.

Here is a poem I wrote to help illustrate the differences between these four negative emotions.

Falling Forward

When I do something wrong, guilt is my friend,
That inner voice whispering, don't do it again.

And then there's regret, who visits me later,
Serving me leftovers, like a judgmental waiter.

Remorse is the dog that continues to bite,
Attacking my peace, all through the night.

Shame is the jury, who won't set me free,
Their verdict was final; the problem "is" me.

So embrace your friend, but don't tip the waiter,
Muzzle the dog and pardon the hater.

Forgive those involved, including yourself,
Remember the lesson and toast to good health.

Never look back at what you left in the grime,
Dust yourself off and continue the climb.

And once you're standing at the top of the slope,
Help others succeed and throw down the rope.

—Chris Harris

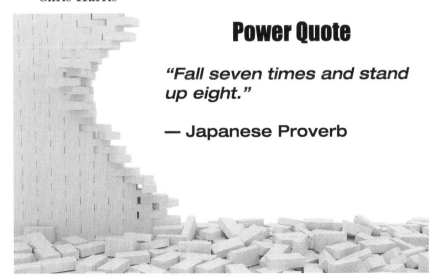

Power Quote

"Fall seven times and stand up eight."

— Japanese Proverb

14: EXPERTS REFRAME

After joining the military, I learned how to march in formation in triple-digit temperatures under a blazing Texas sun. My squadron of 52 men would move in lockstep with one another, around the entire base, while following the authoritative cadence calls of our no-nonsense drill sergeant. The strong smell of our sweat-drenched combat uniforms, which we called fatigues, created a trigger that can take me back to the summer of 1985 faster than the speed of light. Just mix a little body odor with a cotton/nylon-blended fabric and voila, I have my very own time machine! So does this trigger stir up a negative or a positive memory for me?

When I was in the military, I had mixed emotions about whether or not I liked it—at the time. On the one hand, there were lots of reasons to be grateful. Although I didn't make much money, I didn't need much money. Uncle Sam paid for my lodging, clothing, health insurance, and all the food I could shove into my bottomless pit. And, despite the countless jokes surrounding the mess hall, I thought the food was pretty good. The only things I had to pay for were a $7 buzz cut once a month, personal hygiene items, and a bicycle to get around the base (if I didn't want to walk). Eventually, I bought a car and got an apartment in town, but that came later, after I was making better money.

There were also lots of reasons to complain, if one chose to go in that direction. If you didn't like your boss, tough cookies. If you didn't like working the afternoon or graveyard shifts, that was also too bad. Mandatory 12-hour shifts for the entire base, for two weeks straight, because the inspector general was coming to town? This was always a crowd pleaser! The point is, those who chose to be positive remained positive, and those who wanted to gripe and moan did just that. Everyone had a choice to make on how they would frame their military experience, and the narrative they created and chose to embrace became their truth.

Shortly after departing from the military, if a memory wire was tripped that took me back to that season, negative emotions emerged. However, as I began to mature, I changed my narrative to a positive one. I began to tell myself a new story about my time in the military and reframed my experiences with a mat of positivity and a border of gratitude. I exercised my power of choice, and now if someone asks me about that chapter of my life, I refer to it differently. My service to our country got me out of Ohio, gave me a fresh start, and paved the way to a brighter future, which will forever be the story I tell.

Some of my triggers are based on sound, the way Journey's "Don't Stop Believing" takes me back to the ninth grade. Some are based on sight, which is why I turn the other way when I see a Doberman pinscher. And some are based on scent, which is why the smell of Skoal or Copenhagen activates my gag reflex. I have accumulated lots of triggers throughout my life, but I have learned to reframe many of them from a negative to a positive memory. So pick up the pen, put it to paper, and begin the journey of changing which truths you will embrace. After all, you're the architect of your experiences, so reframe the ones you can!

Power Quote

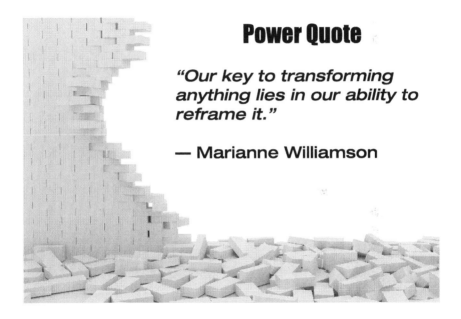

"Our key to transforming anything lies in our ability to reframe it."

— Marianne Williamson

15: EXPERTS SEEK ADVICE

In 1997 I was providing personal safety lectures and self-defense seminars to large companies, like Ernst & Young and American Airlines. I taught elite combatives, both domestically and internationally. And, I had a strong stable of private training students. I had a nice executive office, where I ran the business side of things and taught one-on-one training, but everything else was done at the customer's site. Under this stress-free model, I did what I loved, earned a good living, and my overhead was manageable. The only problem was, all of the A-list instructors had large schools, and I wanted one too.

Although my wife and I had only been married a short while, she knew me well and had a natural gift for business. She was uncomfortable with the idea of trading our lean and efficient business model for a risky one. She advised me to slow down and to bootstrap the idea while scaling in gradually. However, I wanted to start big and chose not to heed her counsel. The next thing I knew, I was locked into a commercial lease with high rent and significant monthly overhead. With three full-time instructors on salary, I found myself having to adopt the same model as other large training centers. This meant lots of day and evening classes, as well as toning down my signature brand of combatives—making it appropriate for children. Teaching kids is the lifeblood of any large school, and it is nearly impossible to survive without them.

Ignoring the advice of others, I leased a 6,000-square-foot training center in Dallas. We had wall lockers, showers, and enough fitness equipment to provide a rigorous, total body workout. There was a row of black leather heavy bags, which hung next to wooden cubbies filled with boxing gloves and sparring gear. We had large mirrors that covered an entire 40-foot wall, as well as 600 square feet of high-density foam mats—to practice ground fighting. Our 12-foot lighted sign bearing our business moniker hung at the top of the two-story brick building. At night it could be seen from several blocks away. The Harris Self-Defense Center was one of the nicest schools in Dallas and was exactly what I wanted—or so I thought. The problem was, running a large facility that was open to the public was robbing me of my joy, causing me to want my former business model back. Eventually, I paid a hefty penalty to buy out of the lease, liquidate the equipment, and close the center altogether. If only I had listened.

Fast-forward 20 years to 2017, when I decided to open another school. But this time I chose to seek counsel from my wife and some business professionals. I had a strong group of black belts in my system that volunteered to help teach, free of charge. I signed a one-year lease on an inexpensive warehouse with very little overhead and offered only three classes per week. And, since I had no employees, the school was paying for itself after the first 90 days.

Because I learned from my previous mistakes, sought sound advice, and kept my expenses low, the entire venture was a wonderful experience and filled with amazing memories. And, when I accepted a promotion at work and decided to close the school, it was a simple and painless process. Learning to ask and choosing to listen made all the difference the second time around. Wisdom surrounds us, but we must choose to embrace it.

Power Quote

"When you make a mistake, there are only three things you should ever do about it: admit it, learn from it, and don't repeat it."

— Bear Bryant

16: EXPERTS RISE TO THE OCCASION

Thinking you have a book in you and actually "writing a book" are two totally different things—I learned this lesson the hard way. In 1999, while living in North Carolina, I received a phone call from a woman in New York City who worked for one of the largest publishers in the world. She explained how she had been tasked with finding the top three self-defense experts in the world and how my name kept coming up during her research. She said they were seeking to publish *The Complete Idiot's Guide to Self-Defense* as the latest book in the *Complete Idiot's Guides* series and wanted to know if I was interested.

After expressing my interest, she promptly requested that I send her my proposed outline and table of contents within the next few business days. To my surprise, I was offered my first book deal. The multi-page contract contained the fine print—including the tight schedule of when each chapter had to be submitted. Hall of Fame catcher Johnny Bench had just co-authored *The Complete Idiot's Guide to Baseball*, and they were adamant about my book following hot on the heels of its release. There would be no allowances for missing deadlines—I was playing in the big leagues now.

The rules were simple: I would be given just over three months to write what would eventually become a 360-page book. My advance would be given in increments, but only as I submitted the agreed upon number of chapters by their corresponding deadlines. If I missed one deadline, I forfeited that portion of the advance. If I missed two deadlines, I forfeited my contract. In all fairness to this wonderful publisher, the conditions were reasonable. The problem was I didn't know how to write a real book.

Having already agreed upon a table of contents, I knew which chapters had to be written and in what order. But trying to work from home with an infant was not productive, so I called a friend who had an office in Raleigh. He generously offered me the use of his space until the project was complete, so I set up a military cot with a sleeping bag, plugged in a mini fridge, and hunkered down for the next few months. It was during this season that I learned how books are really written. It isn't one chapter at a time, one paragraph at a time, or even one sentence at a time. Books are written one word at a time.

Over the next few months, I wrote in four-hour shifts, slept in two-hour shifts, and spent time with my family on Sundays. I only ate when I had to, and I drank lots of caffeine. In addition to writing the book, I was also responsible for providing photos and hiring a professional illustrator, which I paid for with my initial advance. Countless times over the weeks to follow I barraged myself with counterproductive self-talk, like: "Why did you agree to this?" and "What have you gotten yourself into, Harris—you're no writer." Despite feeling like I was in way over my head and desperately wanting to give up, I kept saying out loud: "Chris, this is an opportunity of a lifetime, and you had better rise to the occasion."

I don't know how I made the deadlines, let alone finished the book—but, somehow, I did. The first time I saw my book on the shelf at Barnes & Noble with my name on it, I was consumed with gratitude and a huge sense of relief. Holding my finished work in my hands that day had proven to be its own reward. When opportunity comes knocking—answer the door!

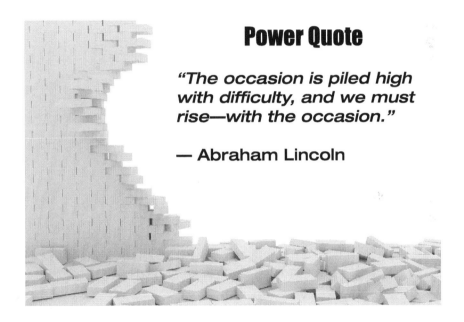

Power Quote

"The occasion is piled high with difficulty, and we must rise—with the occasion."

— Abraham Lincoln

17: EXPERTS UNTIE THE LIE

In Western movies cheating at cards got you shot and stealing cattle got you hanged. The judgments were swift, the penalties were severe, and the offender's only hope of forgiveness or redemption was to find a new town—in another territory.

When my children were smaller, I would say to them: Just because someone lies to you doesn't mean they're a liar, and just because someone steals from you doesn't mean they're a thief. There is a vast difference between someone who "did" something and someone who "is" something. Good people make bad choices, and unless these choices form patterns, we should be careful about labeling because labels stick—sometimes forever.

Growing up, the moment I was in the presence of someone who knew my mother, I would hang my head in shame. Her crimes were printed in the newspapers and reported on the local news, and as a kid, I felt like the world knew. The moment someone identified me as "that woman's son," I could hear the gavel hit the wooden block on the judge's bench. Over time, I became so accustomed to being associated with her sins that I began to label myself—metaphorically wearing a stamp on my forehead that read: "My mother's son."

If we criticize someone enough times (or just one time with enough intensity), we run the risk of our words being repeated in that person's head—a thousand times over. This sobering fact holds true even if our words are founded in lies or misinformation. Has anyone ever said you were ugly, stupid, lazy, or worthless? If so, you had to "accept" it as truth before it "became" truth. And, just as easily as you accepted it—you can reject it. Hurtful words that are carelessly flung out of anger, pain, or ignorance can become the knotted and twisted lies that alter one's self-image and take a lifetime to unravel.

Was it fair for others to judge me for my mother's actions? Was it right? Was it just? Of course not, but what does "fair, right, or just" have to do with it? Anytime someone tells me that life isn't fair, I look them square in the eyes and say, "Compared to what?" To cut myself loose from the lies of my past, I first had to eject the worn-out loop tape I carried on my hip and throw it back into the dark abyss, from where it came. Furthermore, I had to stop feeding, petting, and nurturing the negative opinions of others and take ownership for my part in these two-way affairs. To sum it up: People called me by a name that I didn't like, and I chose to answer to it—plain and simple.

For 20 years I saw myself as the son of a drug dealer. I wore two labels: the one across my back read "not good enough," and the one across my chest read "guilty by association." The good news is, when I made the decision to eject the tape and reject the lies, I was free—in the blink of an eye. Now, reflecting back, it was as if I had voluntarily walked myself into a jail cell as a boy, shut the large metal door behind me, and waited for someone to rescue me—only to realize that I had the key in my pocket the entire time. Self-pity feasts on crumbs, self-doubt thrives without proof, and self-acceptance grows with but a single decision. What ugly lie is living rent free in your head? Are you ready to serve the eviction notice?

Power Quote

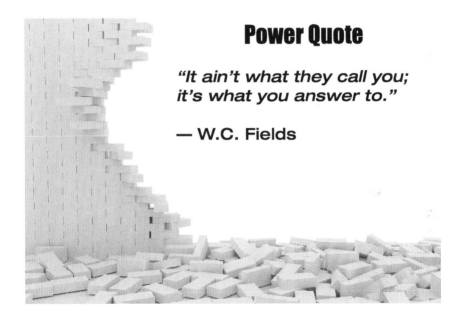

*"It ain't what they call you;
it's what you answer to."*

— W.C. Fields

18: EXPERTS COMPETE WITH THEMSELVES

Martial arts is a highly competitive sport that has more than its share of ego and bravado. It's an industry that thrives on who can beat whom, which system is the best, and who has the baddest instructor. This culture conditioned me to size people up, both mentally and physically, immediately upon meeting them. Practitioners often compare things like the highest kick or the fastest punch, and instructors can sometimes be unrelenting in their pursuit to be better than the dojo around the corner—right down to the pictures on their walls and the trophies on their shelves. Don't get me wrong, there are some great schools that are led by humble instructors who refuse to get caught up in this mindset. And, even though these schools are the crown jewels of the martial arts world, they are also the minority.

During my 20s I experienced a pivotal moment in my life when I finally broke away from this competitive mindset and shifted my focus from "always competing against others" to "only competing against myself." I was living in Oklahoma at the time and training with one of the best "pound-for-pound" kickboxers in the world. The facility was one of the nicest I had ever seen, the training regimen was intense, and the head instructor was dead serious about producing champions. When you showed up, you came to work, without excuse and with very little socializing. I was surrounded by some of the toughest men and women I had ever met. They were gifted athletically, and they poured their blood, sweat, and tears into their dreams of becoming the very best. My reason for being there was completely different. I had a vision of creating my own system of combatives that was a hybrid of the most practical techniques from several different styles, with the hope of one day teaching military groups and the like.

Even though my initial goals were significantly different from my comrades, I found myself becoming consumed with the competitive spirit that surrounded me, and I soon lost track of why I was there. Within a few short months, I became driven to be better than my fellow students. I craved the instructor's approval, I wanted to win every contest, and I had a thirst for acknowledgement that could not be quenched. In short, I lost my focus, forgot my why, and shifted my goals.

Knowing I was completely off track, I arrived at class early one Saturday morning with the intent to sit on the sidelines and silently observe. I wanted to see things from a different perspective and to pinpoint the root of my derailment. Why had I become so focused on winning and so motivated by the praise of others? While sitting cross-legged near the edge of the mat, I came to the stark realization that my identity had been tied to my accomplishments for as long as I could remember. Sadly, my approval of myself had become dependent upon beating others. I was once again in an environment that was fueling this emotional roller coaster, and it was yanking my self-image around each and every turn.

Disappointed by my discovery but encouraged by my resolve, I stood up, gave one final bow of respect toward the instructor and the class, and made a commitment to only compete with myself from that day forward. It pleases me to say that I have successfully kept this commitment and that, in the process, I have become my own fiercest competitor!

Power Quote

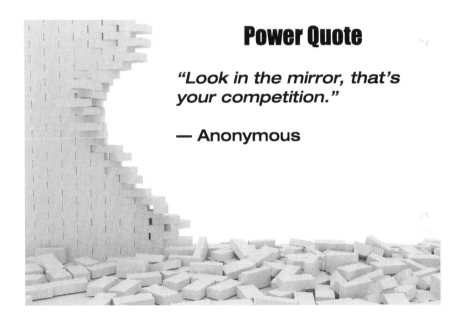

"Look in the mirror, that's your competition."

— Anonymous

19: EXPERTS DO THE LITTLE THINGS

My son attends Texas A&M University in College Station. The Aggie Code of Honor is easy to remember, and most students can recite it by heart: "Aggies do not lie, cheat, or steal, or tolerate those that do." And, although I am 100 percent in agreement with this motto of self-government, I want to take the topic of character and integrity one step further, which I refer to as—the little things. From childhood, most people are taught the big character stuff, like be trustworthy, hardworking, responsible, and loyal. But, in my opinion, it's the little things that truly level the playing field at the end of the day.

One day, after a hard workout at the gym, I witnessed a conversation in the locker room that has always stuck with me. Two men who consistently trained together decided to allow a third guy to join their workout on that particular morning. It was to be an informal evaluation to see if they would let him join their daily regimen, perhaps permanently. And, although the new guy trained with intensity and brought experience to the table, it was quickly decided that they would not allow him to participate in their workouts—ever again. Their reason: Because he chose not to wipe down his treadmill after a brisk run. Apparently, he covered the cardio machine with lots of his sweat but decided not to make the 10-foot journey to the dispenser of sanitized wipes that was mounted on the wall. In short, he didn't clean up after himself. One of the men tried to defend the new guy's behavior by asking his buddy, who had already judged the situation: "So are you saying it's one strike and you're out, no second chances?" The other guy picked up his gym bag and replied: "I've seen all I need to see regarding this guy, he's not joining our group." He then exited the locker room without saying another word. I haven't seen the new guy since.

In the past, when I was seriously considering hiring a person (or working with them), I would invite them to join me at a casual restaurant. I've learned that you can glean a tremendous amount of insight into someone's character over a 45-minute meal, if you pay attention. I look for things like how do they treat the server, table manners, are they buried in their phone, do they offer to pay or thank me when I pay. Do they complain about the food or service or are they positive and complimentary about the experience. Do they say please and thank you. These qualities (or red flags) might never be uncovered during a formal interview, and my "restaurant evaluations" have typically been right.

There's the person who leaves their shopping cart in the middle of the parking lot on a windy day. The one who doesn't put their weights away at the gym, won't replace the toilet paper roll when they use the last of it, or who throws their trash out of the window of their vehicle. I respect and admire those who pick up the piece of trash, especially when it's not their own. The one who runs ahead of the person with the stroller so they can hold the door open. Or, the shopper with a cart full of groceries who lets the person holding a loaf of bread go next. These are my people, and this is my tribe! After all, isn't it the sum of these small, everyday things that add up to the big ones? As they say, it's what you do when nobody's looking, right?

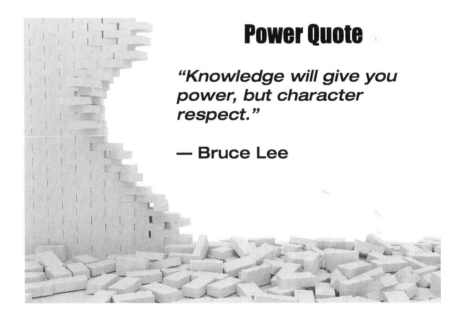

Power Quote

"Knowledge will give you power, but character respect."

— Bruce Lee

20: EXPERTS FIGHT FAIR

My sister Kim was older than I, but not by much. Before we were separated from one another when I was 10 years old, we were great friends. She was tall and skinny for her age, and she was a towhead blond—just like me. She loved to laugh and was always trying to get me to tell her my list of silly jokes, which she'd heard a hundred times. She had an insatiable sweet tooth, so I was always out collecting glass pop bottles and returning them for five cents each so that I could buy Kim her favorite candy.

After we were separated, it was several years before we spoke again. When I was in the military, we would talk on the phone here and there, but always because she needed money. By that point, Kim was knee-deep into her battle with drugs, and her reasons for needing cash were always compelling, and always false. The car won't start, my daughter needs school clothes, I can't make this month's rent—stuff like that. And, although I always sent her money, I knew I was being duped for dope. I justified it in my head by saying, "She's your sister and she needs help." But, in my heart, I knew.

We had only seen each other a handful of times during our adult years, when I received a phone call from Kim while I was living in North Carolina. She said she was sick and needed $2,500 to have some medical tests done. Kim had asked for money countless times over the years, but never for an amount that high. I genuinely wanted to help, if the facts were true, but I wasn't going to give her $2,500 to buy drugs. Conflicted, I told Kim I would be happy to pay the full amount, but I would not give the money to her. I agreed to pay the medical provider directly—I'd put it on my American Express the day an invoice or bill was faxed or emailed to me. There was too much "money history" between us for me to do it any other way.

She began yelling at me over the phone, saying how sick she was and asking why I wouldn't trust her? Sadly, I matched her volume, intensity, and tone, reminding her of her track record as it related to money. Our mouths were firing painful words faster than our brains could filter them. We were both digging into our stockpiles of wounds from our childhood and dragging unrelated issues into the picture—making it impossible to stay on point. Our attacks were getting personal, and we were hitting below the belt. Using generalizations like "always" and "never," we were now in the deep end of the pool. Standing nearby, my wife signaled for me to please end the call and cool down. Taking her advice, I told Kim I needed to go but would call her back later. She refused to answer or return my calls in the future, and that was the last time I ever heard my sister's voice.

Sometime later, I was notified that Kim had just died of cancer and the funeral would be the following day. At the funeral, I learned that doctors had informed her months earlier that she was dying and advised her to go home and get comfortable. But, because of the words we had exchanged over the phone, Kim instructed those who knew of her illness not to notify me, and they respected her wishes. Standing graveside during her funeral on that cold, snowy day in Ohio, all I could think about was what I would give to be able to hug my sister's neck, kiss her on the cheek, muster up one last silly joke, and tell her how much I loved her. Unfortunately, the memories of our last conversation will remain mine to bear. And, although I do not regret my decision surrounding the conditions for giving the money, I would pay a king's ransom to buy one stolen moment—to look my precious sister in the eyes one last time and take back every harsh word ever spoken.

Tomorrow is not promised to anyone, so guard your words carefully—for they can be forgiven, but not forgotten. Be quick to express your love and remain open to forgiveness. Search for opportunities to reconcile—even if it means swallowing your pride. Winning is never as important as we think. And if you have to fight with your words, always fight fair. Life's too short and tomorrow isn't promised.

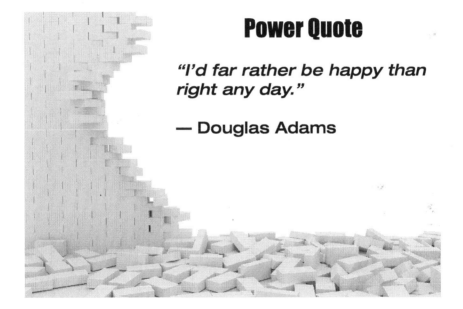

Power Quote

"I'd far rather be happy than right any day."

— Douglas Adams

21: EXPERTS TAKE IT TO THE CAVE

Recently, my family and I were exiting the Dallas/Fort Worth airport with our luggage in tow after a relaxing spring break vacation in the Caribbean. Suddenly, out of nowhere, a young guy, maybe around 18 years old, began violently flinging and dragging an aluminum airport luggage cart. His rage had gotten the best of him, and his anger was out of control. This young man was officially off the rails, and the droves of weary travelers exiting the terminal moved as far away from him as possible, so as not to be physically injured by him or the large metal cart. He was completely oblivious to his surroundings, and it was a miracle that he didn't hurt a small child, or worse. During our shuttle ride home, my wife and kids asked several questions. Why was he acting like that? What was he so angry about? What got him to that breaking point? We each speculated and formed our own hypothesis, but we were only guessing.

Gratefully, I've never lost my temper to the point of putting those around me in physical danger, not even close. But I have blown my top a time or two and blindly flung toxic words toward others, the same way the guy at the airport had violently flung the cart. We've all heard the analogy: The boss takes it out on the employee, the employee takes it out on the spouse, the spouse takes it out on the child, and the child takes it out on the dog. In other words, rather than dealing with our stuff in a healthy and appropriate manner, we repeat the cycle by passing it down the line, until eventually it lands on the lap of someone who won't or can't defend themselves.

Experience has taught me to identify the times when I'm most toxic and take preventative measures to protect others by immediately "taking it to the cave." For me, these increased toxicity levels could be the result of stress, anger, an offense, or a myriad of other reasons. The important thing is that I isolate myself from others until I can properly process my thoughts and emotions and work through them from a safe distance, ensuring that my unfiltered words don't create collateral damage that I will regret later.

By taking it to the cave, I simply withdraw from high-risk scenarios and controversial conversations that require my direct involvement or participation. I find my personal place of solitude, where I can collect my thoughts and reframe any narrative that needs to be converted from a negative to a positive. Also, I let my wife and children know that I'm heading into the cave, so they know that my silence is not personally directed toward them. I have found that communicating openly and honestly with others by telling them that I'm working through something and need a little time and space is definitely the best policy and is usually well received—especially by those who know me best.

My favorite cave is going to the gym and training until my hands are shaking and my clothes are drenched in sweat. My wife's cave is surrounding herself with the sights and sounds of nature. For my daughter, it's her artwork. My son pounds the heavy bag in the garage. Regardless of how you choose to process and reset, the key is self-awareness. By identifying the need to withdraw or retreat early on, we greatly reduce the chances of wounding innocent bystanders with our words or our actions. So, what's your cave?

Power Quote

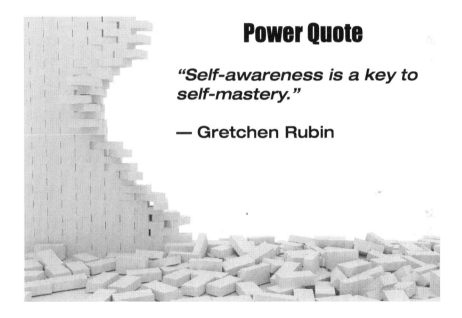

"Self-awareness is a key to self-mastery."

— Gretchen Rubin

22: EXPERTS THINK BEFORE THEY SPEAK

The first requirement for giving advice or honest feedback is to make sure that it's genuinely welcomed. As the saying goes: Unsolicited advice is criticism. Many times, people will ask others for their opinion, but what they really want is an accomplice. Put simply, the person seeking input has already made their decision and is looking for someone who will support it. We must learn to recognize these scenarios and avoid the trap of speaking brutal honesty, when someone is simply searching for a positive word. I have been guilty of this—countless times. My most recent faux pas occurred when Erica, my precious 18-year-old daughter, approached me as I sat in my chair while working. Smiling, she held up her oil painting and asked if I liked it. Most regrettably, after only giving it a quick glance and without thinking, I responded with, "Not really." Instantly, I knew I had wounded my daughter. She is a talented and gifted artist who will go far; I expect her to sell and display her work in prestigious galleries one day. Had I taken the time to understand what she was truly asking, I would have given a response that made her heart glow. Had I closed my laptop and paid attention, I would have seen that she wasn't asking "her father, the art critic." She was asking "daddy, her biggest fan." I would gladly pay a ransom to get those words back.

Unlike the epic fail with my daughter, when someone asks for my opinion, I typically hold my response until I can ask a few questions and understand what is "really" being asked of me. Here are the five things I try to uncover:

Who is asking for the feedback?
Boss, colleague, spouse, child, friend, stranger?

What type of feedback is being asked for?
Honest, brutally honest, affirmation, deep dive?

What level of feedback is being asked for?
A word, sentence, paragraph, page, chapter?

Why does the person want the feedback?
Improvement, approval, accomplice, building a case?

How will the person use the feedback?
Personal, business, public, private, confidential?

Furthermore, I typically do a quick self-evaluation to determine if I'm in the right frame of mind to answer at that moment. Am I stressed? Am I preoccupied or in the middle of a project? Am I pressed for time or under a tight deadline? Sometimes, saying, "Can I put some thought into it and get back with you?" is the best response. Remember, once released, our words cannot be retrieved.

King Abdullah II of Jordan has reigned since 1999 and is a highly accomplished man. As a brigadier general he commanded his country's special forces, and he has trained extensively in the martial arts. Years ago, I was in Amman, the capital city of Jordan, and Abdullah II approached me during a private evening event—to ask for my feedback. Earlier that day, while on the air base, he had witnessed me deliver an intense combatives demonstration surrounding circular joint manipulation. He now wanted my opinion regarding a system of combatives he was evaluating, with the possibility of integrating it into his existing training program. Standing directly in front of me, and surrounded by his armed security detail, he stopped talking, looked me in the eyes, and awaited my response. I knew of the system he was asking me about, and I had a strong opinion on the matter—but should I answer or keep my mouth shut? After weighing the situation carefully, I chose to respond by asking for his opinion on the matter, which he gladly offered. Afterward, a member of his security team whispered in his ear, and he was gone. Should I have given this powerful leader my opinion in this situation? I guess I'll never know.

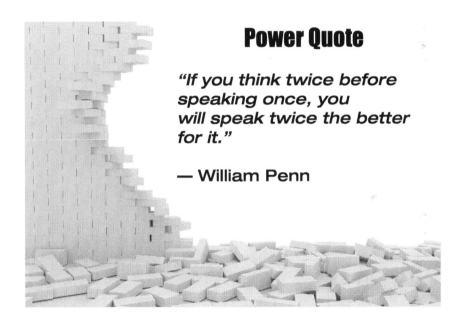

Power Quote

"If you think twice before speaking once, you will speak twice the better for it."

— William Penn

23: EXPERTS PROTECT THEIR ASSETS

Health and wellness are life's greatest assets and should remain at the top of our list of priorities—at all times. When combined, our health and wellness make up our state of mind, state of living, and state of being—creating the proverbial wellspring of life. To effectively guard these invaluable treasures, we must first master the art of protecting our time, energy, and mindset—leading us to a balanced life.

I was 43 years old when I moved back to the United States after living in Central America for two years while doing humanitarian work. While I immersed myself into the constant needs of the children and employees at the orphanage, I neglected nearly every aspect of my health. Once back in Texas, I was exhausted, both mentally and physically. I felt fat, tired, and weak. I was too young to feel so old. As a master combatives instructor, it was considered unacceptable for a warrior to "let themselves go," yet something as simple as walking up the stairs caused me to become out of breath. Embarrassed and fed up with myself, I decided to make my personal wellbeing my number one priority. Within 48 hours of being back in the U.S., I joined a gym, hired a trainer and dietician, and set a goal of getting fit.

To achieve my goal, the first thing I had to do was find a way to physically exercise on a daily basis. But, since energy and motivation had to be achieved before anything else, I started with my diet. Being out of sorts and out of shape, I had become dependent on carbohydrates and 24-ounce energy drinks to get through each day. Depriving myself of my carb and caffeine addiction was a miserable experience in the beginning—but it had to be done. During the first two weeks I dreamt about pasta and potatoes.

I eliminated sugar, then processed foods, then fried foods and white flour. After incorporating lots of raw fruits and vegetables, I eventually found myself with enough get-up-and-go to begin exercising again. Until I hit my fitness goals, food was to be viewed as nothing more than fuel. There would be no eating for pleasure while in training mode. Once I was energized and motivated to do the work (thanks to a disciplined diet), I needed to find the time to exercise.

Experience has taught me that when it comes to exercise, you don't find the time—you make the time. I tried lots of different formulas, but the one that worked best for me was disciplining myself to wake up 90 minutes earlier than I needed to and using that time to go to the gym. By reserving each morning for "health and fitness time" and setting clear boundaries to protect it, I began to reap the rewards of paying myself first. Each month I lifted more weight, did more reps, and increased my cardio.

While training my body, I simultaneously trained my mindset. First, I avoided any type of media that intentionally promoted or created fear—because fear creates doubt and doubt is the archenemy of progress. Second, I distanced myself from negative and pessimistic people. Third, anytime I was driving or exercising, I only listened to music and audiobooks that inspired and encouraged me. If my mindset became corrupted, my diet would follow suit, then my energy, then my consistency. Mindset is king!

Within 18 months I fully restored my mental and physical health; I became stronger and had more vitality than when I was in my 30s. By creating the necessary boundaries to protect my greatest assets, I got in the best shape of my adult life. Time, energy, and mindset are the gateways to peace, fulfillment, and personal well-being—so let's guard them like our quality of life depends on it.

100

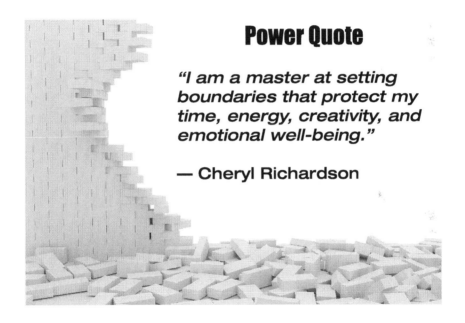

Power Quote

"I am a master at setting boundaries that protect my time, energy, creativity, and emotional well-being."

— Cheryl Richardson

24: EXPERTS FIND A WAY TO LET IT GO

One of the foster families I lived with as a boy had an adult son who was still living at home at the time. He was an obese 19-year-old, weighing well over 300 pounds, and he enjoyed tormenting me every chance he could get. His favorite thing to do was to sit on me while pinning my wrists to the ground, above my head, as I squirmed and screamed frantically, trying to escape. He always laughed while doing this. I couldn't have weighed more than 80 pounds at the time and was extremely claustrophobic—so being trapped under a bully of his size was a terrifying experience. His reasoning for his behavior was as twisted as he was. He "claimed" he was doing me a favor by breaking me of my claustrophobia. It would take several years to get the stench of his body odor out of my nostrils.

Thirty years later, I was attending my sister's funeral in Ohio. She had died at 44 years old, and I flew to Dayton for the memorial service. All of a sudden, and out of nowhere, the bully who had scarred me three decades earlier stepped up to the podium, opened his Bible, and began to pray. I was speechless and in shock. I felt as if I was going to throw up, pass out, or both. My mind was flooded with questions, like: "What in the hell is this man doing at my sister's funeral?" "How dare he pretend to be a Pastor!" "Stop praying over my sister, you freaking hypocrite!" I was not prepared to bury my sister before her 45th birthday, and I most definitely wasn't prepared to see this man from my past officiating the service. It took everything in me to hold it together.

Concluding the service, he put his black leather Bible under his arm and headed straight for me. I wanted to throw a forearm to his face and knock him out cold! The only thing that stopped me was "where I was" and "why I was there." Putting his hand on my shoulder, he whispered these words in my ear: "All that stuff is water under the bridge; you need to let it go." I thought:

"Wait, what? Is this supposed to be some sick, twisted apology or something?" Without saying a word, I turned around and walked out the door to pull myself together.

For the entire journey back to Dallas, his cavalier comment was all I could think about. There was a loop tape playing in my head, and I didn't know how to make it stop. For years, I have been unconditionally forgiving people who had never asked for it. This was one of my expert powers and the currency I used to purchase my freedom. But this was different. This man had basically told me to get over it while offering no apology, and at my sister's funeral. I was deeply offended, and I didn't want to let it go.

After weeks of internal conflict, I made a pivotal decision. I wrote down on a sheet of paper every infraction connected to my offense toward this man, including his final words to me. Then, I put my grievances in a sealed envelope with the words "GRAVE OFFENSE" written on it, threw it in a fire, and watched it burn. By permanently destroying the evidence of this long-standing offense, I found my way to let it go, once and for all.

Power Quote

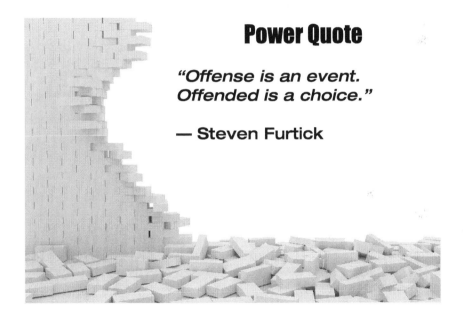

*"Offense is an event.
Offended is a choice."*

— Steven Furtick

25: EXPERTS ARE HUMBLE

In 2011 I was one of only 40 international applicants selected to conduct a dynamic demonstration at the Non-Lethal Capabilities Show in Ottawa, Canada. This live demo was conducted inside a heated tent at the Connaught Ranges, with temperatures peaking at 40 degrees Fahrenheit and a brisk wind that rattled the canvas the entire day. The event was sponsored by NATO and jointly hosted by the U.S. Department of Defense Non-Lethal Weapons Program and the Canadian Department of National Defence. The purpose was to showcase new capabilities that could be acquired and fielded quickly, in support of the International Security Assistance Force (ISAF) and counterterrorism operations in Afghanistan. High-ranking government officials and decorated military leaders from several countries were in attendance, as well as key decision-makers from important security-related sectors.

I hoped to secure new contracts for a patented control and restraint device I had invented and for my signature combatives program. This meant I had to take someone with me who could withstand a full day of joint manipulation and forceful takedowns, which required a great deal of skill and stamina. I had the perfect warrior in mind—his name was Doug Iedema. Doug and I had met 18 months earlier through a men's group at a local church and immediately became friends. His stout linebacker physique was just as strong as his character. He had a background in mixed martial arts (MMA), an abnormally high tolerance for pain, and he could really take a punch (and give one). And, Doug was a highly capable instructor who had helped me teach combatives on numerous occasions.

As a result of our efforts, we caught the attention of one of the top special forces instructors from Israel, whom I shall refer to as Jax—as a professional courtesy. Impressed by what he saw, Jax and one of his fellow instructors flew to Dallas a few months after our initial meeting in Canada. The purpose of their visit was to go through a grueling 10-hour training course with Doug and me. A friend of mine gave me the keys to his Krav Maga school for the entire day, where we closed the blinds, locked the doors, and went to work.

Although I had served in the military as a young man, I had never earned the privilege of being in the special forces, but I had trained them on occasion and knew what to expect. As an active team member of the Israeli Special Forces, as well as an instructor, Jax was relentless throughout the day. Drill after drill, he proved to be one of the toughest men we had ever met. He had several thick scars where knives and bullets had entered and exited his body, sometimes passing through the bone. And, although his skill set and work ethic were utterly impressive, what stopped us in our tracks was his genuine humility.

I have always aspired to be humble but often fall short of the goal. I model it some of the time, but never consistently. Insecurity? Pride? Seeking approval? These are the questions I ask myself when my arrogance rears its head and I want to know why. I view humility as "accepting my value and self-worth as a constant but viewing my importance as being situational." Jax was one of the best in the world at his craft; he exemplified a life filled with heroic deeds—yet he remained humble. By his example, I found myself inspired and determined to continue my pursuit of this most admirable quality.

Power Quote

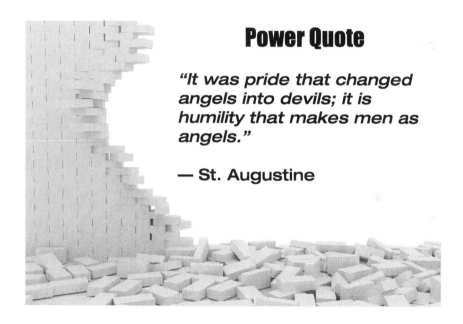

"It was pride that changed angels into devils; it is humility that makes men as angels."

— St. Augustine

26: EXPERTS DON'T MAKE IT PERSONAL

As a veteran inventor, new ideas always seem to come to me at the most inconvenient times, and the middle of the night is no exception. Several years back, I was suddenly awakened at 3 a.m. with a detailed vision I had for a new personal safety product. Without hesitation I jumped out of bed and stumbled down the hall toward my desk to find a pen and paper. One crucial lesson that experience has taught me over the years is the importance of writing down a new inspiration the moment it comes calling, even if this meant stepping out of a meeting, pulling the vehicle over on the side of the road, or jumping out of bed at zero-dark-30.

Having numerous patents under my belt and knowing several colleagues who invent as a pastime or profession, I admit that one of our greatest downfalls is becoming entirely too attached to our ideas, to the point of seeing them as our babies and referring to them as a part of us. Once this mental shift happens and we make that little spark of genius something personal, we lose the ability to view and evaluate the project and product objectively, which opens the doors to an onslaught of unforgiving mistakes.

I learned this lesson the hard way. With an interested buyer for this idea actively pursuing me, I decided to be difficult and uncooperative. I wasn't after more money; the truth was, I was too close to the invention. I simply couldn't let it go. It was mine; I gave birth to it; I developed it from scratch. How could I sell my brainchild to the highest bidder? Meanwhile, back in the real world, the bills were stacking up quickly. In the end, the buyer got weary, lost interest, and moved on—and there was nobody else standing in line.

What should have been a very profitable venture, and put my life on a new trajectory, ended as a huge financial loss with a product that ended up going nowhere. This was the day that I made an invaluable course correction: I decided to detach from my ideas the same way a builder detaches from a house when it's ready to sell. Moving forward, I would no longer make my ideas personal. Instead, I would follow a sound and strategic methodology by building prototypes that proved the concept, filing for the patent, and once approved, selling the patent. Furthermore, I would strive to target buyers who had the resources, experience, and network needed to succeed in the marketplace.

Don't get me wrong, there's a time for experts, such as writers, artists, designers, or musicians, to create solely for the love of their craft. What I'm referring to is not making things personal when the goal is to put food on the table. The day I began viewing my inventions as a business was the day that my business became profitable. For me, comingling my passion with the need to provide for my family has become a thing of the past, and I now have a deeper understanding of what Thomas Edison meant when he said, "Anything that won't sell, I don't want to invent." Based on his comment, I believe Mr. Edison learned this lesson too.

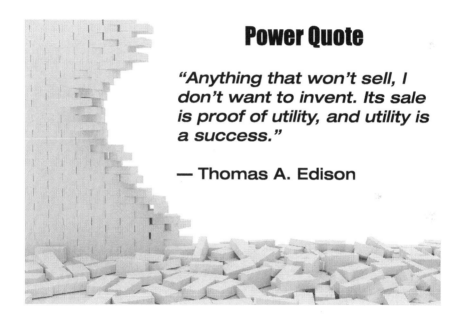

Power Quote

"Anything that won't sell, I don't want to invent. Its sale is proof of utility, and utility is a success."

— Thomas A. Edison

27: EXPERTS MOVE ON

Several years ago, my wife and I enjoyed a fabulous dinner at an upscale restaurant, followed by an expensive bottle of champagne and the clinking of crystal glasses. I had just sold the U.S. patent to one of my inventions, and we were celebrating. I transferred all of the rights to my intellectual property to the buyer in exchange for a down payment, a promissory note for the remaining balance, and a royalty for each unit sold. It was the best of times. Or was it? Trying to save money, I hired an inexpensive attorney to represent my side of the negotiations, with the buyer's attorney drafting the contracts and agreements. My frugality would cost me a small fortune, as I missed one crucial point in the end. There should have been language stating that "all rights would revert to me" if the remaining balance was not paid in full by a specified date. Unfortunately, the remaining balance was never paid, the buyer kept my valuable patent, and I chose to play the role of the victim for the next few months.

I felt cheated! Not only did I have countless hours invested in this invention, but I was also banking on its success to contribute to my family's financial future. With signed contracts in hand, we naively believed it was a done deal and began to dream about a brighter, more secure future. We talked about helping those in need, a fund for the kids, investment strategies, and international travel. And, to make matters worse, my wife and I put earnest money down on a new home, with a closing date scheduled around our big payday. We chose the colors, flooring, cabinetry, and light fixtures—taking emotional ownership of the house. Six different times, the final payout for the patent got pushed back, always due to some unforeseen circumstances. My wife was the first to accept the fact that we had been burned and that the money and patent were both gone. It would take me much longer to accept this truth.

After we canceled the contract for the new house, I decided to meet with a reputable attorney—I wanted to know my options. After reviewing the documentation, the attorney was confident of our chances of winning in court. But we would have to sue the buyer, which would consume a great deal of time and money, not to mention the stress it would create. I had been bamboozled, and I was furious! I wanted this company to either pay me my money—or give me my patent back.

By choosing to play the victim of a "deal gone bad," I became critical and pessimistic. Sadly, I was wallowing in self-pity and poisoning the environment around me with negativity—becoming that person who always complains about the same thing. I was that guy you see at the gym—and turn the other way. Disappointed in myself, I looked at my wife one day and said, "No more!" I decided to cut my losses, accept the fact that the money and patent were gone forever, and not to file a lawsuit. It was time to let it go, put it in the past, and move on—which is exactly what I did. I'm excited to say that I'm inventing again, and my next patent is coming soon.

Power Quote

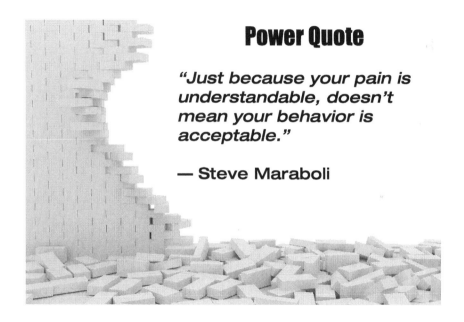

"Just because your pain is understandable, doesn't mean your behavior is acceptable."

— Steve Maraboli

28: EXPERTS SHOW MERCY

At roughly 12 years old, I lived with a man and his wife at the time (I believe she was his fourth). By day, he worked downtown as a counselor. By night, he drank Budweiser and lots of it. He was a little guy, genetically lean with good muscle tone—and he always wore a white sleeveless T-shirt in the evenings. He had a thick head of wavy brown hair and a neatly groomed mustache and beard; he looked just like Clint Eastwood in *The Outlaw Josey Wales* movie (which I think he did on purpose). He carried a large chip on his shoulder, and if anyone called him short, he would be up in their face like a hot-headed coach over a bad call during a championship game.

He had taken it upon himself to "toughen me up" and "make me into a man" by hitting me and slapping me around whenever he was drunk enough and the mood struck him. His physical abuse never seemed to hurt that much, mainly because of his size and because he packed a weak punch. But being bullied by an adult angered me greatly. He owned a one-year-old Doberman pinscher that he bought for protection and trained to attack on command. He found it entertaining to watch the dog corner me in fear while baring her razor-sharp teeth and issuing a deep, guttural growl. I wasn't afraid of the drunk, but I was terrified of the dog. During his stupors, I would sometimes tell him that one day he was going to have to fight me as a man—and he wasn't going to like it. He would always laugh at my brave declaration but, though I was 12, I was serious. Eventually, Social Services showed up to haul me off to my next home, and as we drove away, I promised under my breath that I would return—as a man.

Immediately upon finishing my time in the Air Force, I moved back to Dayton for a season to figure out my next move. I was 22 years old, very well trained, and in the best shape of my life. It was only my third day back in town when

I decided to make good on my word from 10 years earlier. It was time to give the mean drunk a visit and to settle the score. Unannounced, I arrived on his covered front porch on a warm afternoon. The purpose of my visit was simple: I was there to serve justice. Looking through the busted screen door as I knocked repeatedly, I saw the Doberman from my past lying in the entryway. Grossly overweight and looking like an old sack of potatoes, she was no longer the threatening attack dog of her youth.

The look on the man's face when he saw me standing there, towering over him, was epic. I simply said, "Remember me?" and I thought he was going to wet himself. His expression seemed one part fear, one part panic, and one part guilt. I reveled in the silence while his eyes darted back and forth, searching his outdated database for a safe response. I was there to kick his ass, and he knew it. Staring him down as he nervously tried to find his words, I suddenly became overwhelmed with a sense of pity. I felt sorry for him. His face was worn from decades of alcohol abuse, and his deep wrinkles were like road maps to a life of unresolved pain. Standing there with my power, the look on his face and the fear in his heart proved to be enough. So, without saying another word, I turned around, walked away, and got on with my life. I chose mercy.

Power Quote

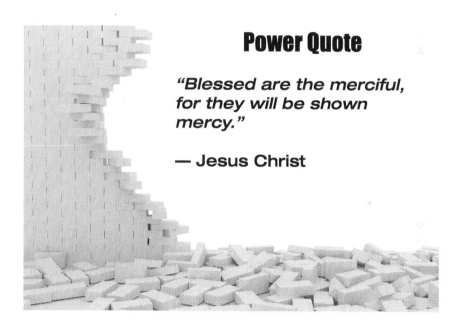

"Blessed are the merciful, for they will be shown mercy."

— Jesus Christ

29: EXPERTS KNOW THEIR VALUES

If you want to change your character, change your habits.

If you want to change your habits, change your actions.

If you want to change your actions, change your thoughts.

If you want to change your thoughts, change your beliefs.

Our beliefs are the foundation that supports the house, the roots that anchor the tree, and the rudder that steers the ship. It is from our beliefs that we derive our values—and from our values that we derive our standards. The bottom line is, if you want to know what someone believes, look at their character.

My mother wasn't always a drug addict. At one point, she was a beautiful and vivacious woman—full of hopes and dreams. I will always remember the day that she met the man who introduced her to the world of drugs. The choices that she made on that day changed her life, my life, and the lives of my two sisters—forever. Within a few short months she evolved from being a recreational drug user, to a drug addict, to a drug dealer—just like that. When she met this man, her belief system was weak, resulting in her conforming her values (or lack thereof) to that of her environment. When our foundation is weak and when our root system is malnourished, bad company will do what it does best: corrupt good character. Standing on the sidelines as a child, I witnessed this painful chain of events unfold; I learned several life lessons that I will never forget. Firstly, I learned that with no clearly defined values in place, we are highly exposed and extremely vulnerable—with no fences or walls to protect us. Secondly, I learned the vital importance of setting firm boundaries with regard to the personal and professional influences we allow in our lives. This includes

acquaintances, friends, colleagues, and most importantly—
leaders.

I cannot overemphasize the importance of surrounding
ourselves with the right people. I have acquaintances, and I
have friends—and I have come to know the difference. For me
to consider someone a true friend—someone I want to navigate
life with—I prefer that we align in both interests and values,
and that's not always an easy combination to find. I choose
to surround myself with people who set high standards for
themselves and who prioritize those standards—those with a
code, if you will. And, when they're hit with the storms of life
or when mistakes are made, they stand firm at the helm like
any good captain—adjusting their sails and making course
corrections wherever necessary. With friends, I don't seek
perfection—I simply look for people who know their values and
do their best to stay the course.

Have you ever worked for someone who managed from
their beliefs and values? In my lifetime, I have worked with
lots of different managers and leaders—some bad, some good,
and some who were great. I've always considered the men and
women who used their positional power to "coerce or reward"
performance as less than impressive—at least in my book. I rate
the ones who "led by example" as good—sometimes even great.
And, on a few occasions, I have had the privilege to work with
leaders who inspired and motivated others from the depths of
their values and with their genuine expert power—these were
the exceptional few! One leader who stands out is Brad Hansen.
Working with Brad for several years, I witnessed firsthand the
incredible power of "values-based leadership," and how he used
his natural authenticity and unyielding convictions to transform
the lives of those he led. And, he did so while creating a culture
of trust, respect, and efficiency. So how did the core values of
one individual have such a positive and significant impact on
so many? The answer is simple: Strong values are infectious,

and people want to follow that which is true and just. We want lights, not trumpets. We crave the Brads. During our lives, the most important compass we possess is our moral compass—so always protect it and let it lead the way.

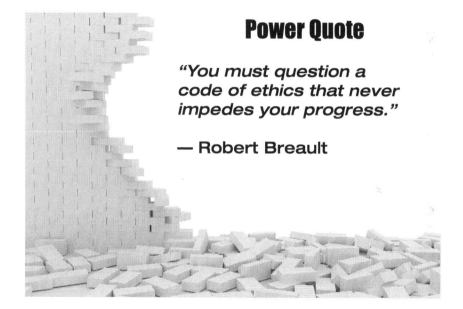

Power Quote

"You must question a code of ethics that never impedes your progress."

— Robert Breault

30: EXPERTS BET ON THEMSELVES

When you teach close quarters combat for a living, every contract counts. Therefore, each offer to bid on a job has to be taken with the utmost seriousness. High-level combatives training was, and still is, a feast-or-famine business, with no guarantees as to when the phone will ring next.

Several years ago, I was living in Dallas when I got a call from Jacob, who was my Arab Gulf States sponsor. I was always excited to hear from him because it generally meant I was about to go to work. Jacob called to inform me that we had just received an invitation to bid on a government tender in the Gulf States region and wanted to know if I was interested. However, he cautioned me to listen to all of the details before giving my answer, due to the potential for serious physical injury and the risk of financial loss. This meant I would have to be willing to bet on myself, with no promise of gain.

In total, only five invitations were sent out to candidates, each of whom met a specific list of qualifications. The rules were simple: To compete, each person had to arrive at an Allied Military Base in the region on a prescheduled date. Once there, we would have to fight the existing master combatives instructor, whose three-year contract was about to expire. The bottom line—they wanted the best and would accept no substitutions.

This bare-handed, no-pads showdown would have no refs, no rounds, and no rules, and it was to take place in a room filled with several high-ranking military officials and a member of their country's royal family. The incumbent was a seasoned expert from Western Asia, who desperately wanted his contract renewed and was determined to keep his job, since he sent his wages back home to support his impoverished family. Put simply, I would be fighting for my livelihood, but he would be fighting for survival. Aside from the risk of being seriously injured, we each had to pay our own travel expenses. For me, it would cost $5,000 for a 16,000-mile roundtrip journey, which would only be reimbursed if I won.

After arriving, I learned that two of the five men invited had declined to make the trip altogether, and the other two had already fought and lost, meaning it was down to just me. At the base, I was ushered into a large executive conference room with polished tile floors and elaborate furnishings. The moment I walked in, everyone stood up and formed a circle around me and my opponent as we "toed the line," only inches apart. In my mind I was thinking, "There's no way in hell I'm getting stuck with a $5,000 American Express bill—I am going to win!" With no fanfare, small talk, or introductions, a colonel shouted "FIGHT," and after a few aggressive clashes, I successfully breached his dominant blind side and within two seconds I had him tightly locked in a standing rear naked choke—the match was over.

Looking back, it's hard to believe that in less than a minute I had earned the contract, solidified a new level of trust and respect with my sponsor, and changed my stars. This victory elevated my career to a new level, resulting in more training deals in the future. For the rest of my days, I will always refer to this pivotal moment of my career as "the time I bet on myself!"

Power Quote

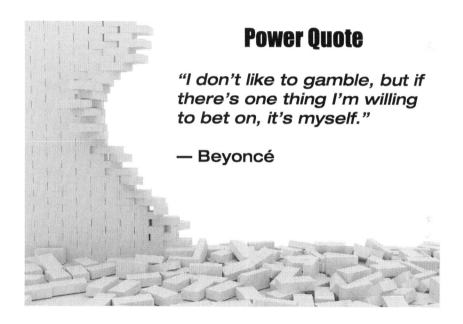

"I don't like to gamble, but if there's one thing I'm willing to bet on, it's myself."

— Beyoncé

31: EXPERTS PASS IT ON

Do you have a gift, talent, or expert power that you have passed on to another person? If so, you have taken an important step toward duplicating that unique part of yourself and planted the seeds for it to evolve beyond you. This is a wonderful way to leave behind an inheritance with your fingerprint on it. We learn something; we share it; we watch it grow.

I spent years developing a system of close quarters combat, which I named Roku Jutsu. Roku is the Japanese word for the number six. Jutsu means method. I chose this name because of the six different styles (or methods) of martial arts I trained in throughout my journey. My goal was to select 60 of the most practical techniques and create a method of combatives specifically designed for law enforcement and military groups. For a technique to be selected, it had to be easy to learn, simple to execute, and highly effective, aligning with our core philosophy of "less is more, less is better." To obtain a black belt in Roku Jutsu, a student must perform all 60 techniques proficiently and instinctively, without exception. They then must successfully defend themselves against 20 consecutive attacks from a black belt, at full speed, and with extreme intensity.

When I began teaching professionally back in 1993, I called the system by a different name, but the training was the same. During the 26 years since, I have trained thousands of students through classes, seminars, assemblies, and private training. However, only 26 individuals have earned the esteemed rank of black belt in Roku Jutsu. When training civilians, I have a very simple requirement: Their character and maturity must be proportionate to the level of skill they are seeking. To whom much is given, much will be required, which is why I have always been selective about whom I teach. I refuse to teach hotheads, bullies, those seeking revenge, and people with something to prove. Once you pass a professional skill set on to someone, you can never take it back—so choose wisely.

Each of these 26 black belts has proven themselves on the mat, where it counts most. I will never forget Shelbi Parker. Still in college and weighing less than a hundred pounds, she was determined to be the first woman to earn our highest rank. So, in a room surrounded by men who had already made the journey, she persevered, with relentless determination and inspiring fortitude. During her test, we metaphorically bled with her, cried with her, and suffered each hit with her—especially the punch that broke her glasses, sending them flying across the room. But most importantly, we all experienced victory— through her. On that day, Shelbi shared her newly acquired expert power with everyone in the room, and what she gave to us can never be lost or taken away. My greatest desire when training a student is to make them better than I am. On that day, Shelbi's indomitable spirit surpassed all of ours, leaving us with a tremendous sense of pride and accomplishment. Now, I enthusiastically observe from the sidelines, as students like Shelbi pass their power on to others—advancing lives in the process.

Do you paint? Can you play an instrument? Are you great with numbers? Can you build a website or coach a sport? Whatever your expert power is, whatever your passion is, find someone with an ear to listen and a desire to learn—and begin making the transfer. Find a way to replicate your greatest strengths in the lives of those who are eager to do the work— and watch what happens!

Power Quote

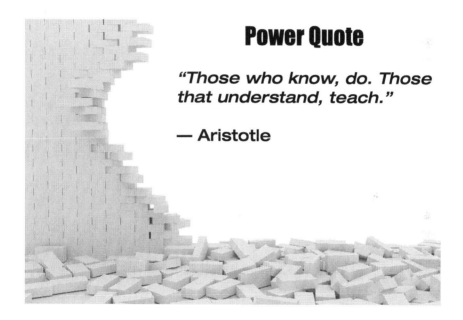

"Those who know, do. Those that understand, teach."

— Aristotle

32: EXPERTS TAKE RISKS

In 2000 I opened my first trading account so I could buy a few hundred shares of stock from a company that had caught my interest. I downloaded the broker's online trading platform, bought my shares, and was officially hooked on trading. The hunt, the strategy, the upside potential—I loved it all! Hungry to learn more, I began attending various day-trading schools throughout the U.S., each ranging from a few days to a few weeks in length, all of which were expensive. In the beginning, I tried my hand at stocks, the indexes, and options. After a few years of bouncing around, I finally settled on the Foreign Exchange Market (Forex), where I traded the exchange rate fluctuations between currency pairs of select countries. Forex is the largest and most liquid market in the world, and the fact that it is active 24 hours per day and only closed on weekends made it the ideal trading vehicle for my busy schedule.

Eager to learn, I took my laptop with me everywhere I went so I could capitalize on windows of downtime by studying the market and watching the charts. Airports, hotels, Chick-fil-A, even on my recumbent bike—it didn't matter. I was determined to earn my expert power in this new endeavor and willing to do the work. In the beginning, it was an emotional and financial roller coaster ride. I would make money, then give it right back. As a rookie, it was a journey of one step forward and two steps back—but I knew I would eventually figure it out and was committed to seeing it through.

To become a successful trader, I had to learn risk management, conquer my fear of financial loss, and work through the "trading psychology" stuff that affects all beginners. New traders are notorious for letting their losers run long and for cutting their winners short, and it was no different for me at first. Uptrends were driven by greed, downtrends by fear, and whipsaws were fueled by the battles between the two.

Whipsaws are volatile swings that buck the prices up and down, like an angry bronco at a sold-out rodeo that constantly throws rookie traders off its back. Those who learn when to enter, when to exit, and when to stay out, are rewarded with their very own expert power, providing them with the ability to earn money from a laptop anywhere with Wi-Fi. Those who are thrown into the dirt too many times pack up their saddlebags and leave the arena of trading for good.

I eventually became a skilled trader and earned very consistent profits, which evolved into me trading other people's money, as well as my own. But I was not properly conditioned "mentally" for the significant increase of profit, loss, or risk—causing me to become overly cautious and to second-guess myself. This resulted in the resurgence of costly rookie mistakes. The fear of losing large amounts of other people's money with a single trade affected my self-discipline, which had become the cornerstone of my success. And, when I began ignoring my list of strict rules, which was framed on my desk as well as committed to memory, I decided to close the master account altogether. I had gone way too big, way too fast, and concluded that if I were ever going to trade the wealth of others, I would need to ease into it gradually. In the meantime, I would take a step back and focus on my own account, at least for now.

Taking educated risks is crucial to our growth and vital to our success. In fact, many of the personal stories in this book are the direct result of times when I bet largely on myself. And, looking back, I only regret the bets that didn't teach me something valuable (and I've learned from all of them). I firmly believe that the bold are the ones who truly live, and that fortune really does favor the bold. So, what would you do if you knew you couldn't fail? Don't let the fear of loss or disappointment stand in your way. We are resilient, we are brilliant, and we have been built for risk!

Power Quote

"Life should not be a journey to the grave with the intention of arriving safely in a pretty and well-preserved body, but rather to skid in broadside in a cloud of smoke, thoroughly used up, totally worn out, and loudly proclaiming 'Wow! What a ride!'"

— Hunter S. Thompson

33: EXPERTS KNOW THEIR AUDIENCE

In 2012 I was teaching at the Marine Corps Air Combat Center, known as Twentynine Palms, located in the Mohave Desert in Southern California. I was conducting an advanced hand-to-hand combat class to a group of 16 Marines, two of whom were certified Martial Arts Instructor-Trainers. These highly qualified soldiers would be evaluating my skill set for an after-action report they would send up the chain of command. Then it would be determined if I would be invited to teach my course at Quantico Marine Corps Base in Virginia—to a more senior group.

The evaluation of my performance at Twentynine Palms was well received by a military colonel in Virginia, and the date was set for me to teach at Quantico. The class size was limited to 30 participants, many of whom were certified trainers for their respective groups or agencies. In attendance were instructors from the FBI, Secret Service, Federal Air Marshal Service, and Marine Corps Martial Arts Program. They were a seasoned group of highly trained professionals, with hundreds of years of collective field and combat experience. It was a privilege to be in the same room with these experts, and there would be no room for mistakes from my end. We covered a great deal of material, including instinctive reactions, control and restraint, joint manipulation, and how to quickly escape lateral vascular neck restraints. In addition to the physically demanding portion of the training, I lectured on the central nervous system (CNS) and reflex arc, as well as the fight-or-flight stress response and how it relates to the release of adenosine triphosphate (ATP). The training was 70 percent physical and 30 percent lecture-based.

At the end of the class, I asked a high-ranking Marine Corps officer, who had been observing the training, if he would do something for me. I kindly requested that he provide me with an evaluation of my overall performance after he had a chance to get feedback from the participants. I encouraged him to be brutally honest and not hold any punches—because I wanted to find ways to improve the quality of the program. He shook my hand firmly and gladly agreed.

Approximately one month later, I received the Marine Corps officer's honest feedback. And, true to his word, he gave it to me straight—right between the eyes. Paraphrasing, I will do my best to summarize his critique. After getting past the pleasantries, he said if I had taken the time to get to know my audience, by doing my homework on the front end, I would have definitely chosen another topic for the lecture portion. The men and women attending the training were very well versed on the topic of CNS, reflex arc, fight-or-flight, and ATP. And, some found it insulting that I was teaching them a subject that they knew more about than I did. In fact, several of the attendees taught this stuff—ouch!

For the next few weeks, I kicked myself hard. I had been confident I had done an exceptional job and that the evaluation would be positive. Now all I could think about was how ridiculous I must have looked, lecturing down to these subject-matter experts—on material they knew inside and out. I was embarrassed, my pride was wounded, and I struggled to let it go. But, eventually, I decided to learn from my mistakes, and I am now committed to always being prepared, in advance. From that day forward, I became serious about truly knowing my audience—and my training programs are better for it.

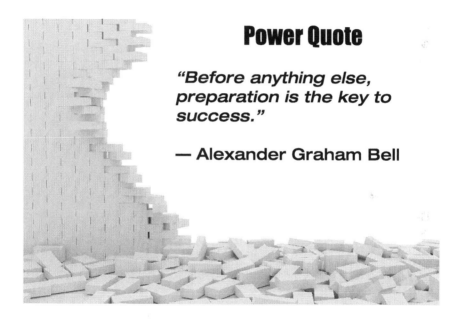

Power Quote

"Before anything else, preparation is the key to success."

— Alexander Graham Bell

34: EXPERTS PRACTICE GRATITUDE

During a short but important trip to India, I encountered a laundry list of negative experiences. I had just arrived with my sponsor and had a very busy schedule over the days to follow—with very little downtime. Upon landing, it took nearly three hours to get through customs, causing us not to get checked in to the Hilton until 2 a.m., and we had an important meeting in the morning. Just after sunrise, my sponsor phoned my room to tell me he was feeling sick and would not be going with me. I had the concierge hail a cab and headed out on my own.

It was hot and muggy, with 100 percent humidity, and since the AC in my room was not working, I didn't sleep a wink during the few hours I lay in bed. And now, sitting in the backseat of a 20-year-old black and yellow taxi, my anxiety began to rise. Stuck in the worst traffic jam I had ever experienced, I tried to keep calm. We remained at a complete standstill on the eight-lane Western Express Highway for three grueling hours. To make matters worse, I had to roll up the window because it started to rain. I did not make the meeting.

Arriving back at the Hilton, I was met by my sponsor, who was livid. Even though he had been sick and couldn't go with me, he was upset that I had not met with the client, which led to an uncomfortable discussion before dinner. Sleep deprived, overheated, and hungry, I decided to keep my mouth shut and order my food. Once the waiter set my plate in front of me, I immediately snatched the long, slender pepper that was sitting on top of the bed of rice and shoved it in my mouth. I was famished and had not thought it through, and within a minute, I knew I had made a terrible mistake. My eyes began to water profusely, and my tongue felt like it was melting. It was the hottest thing I had ever eaten, and it took six pieces of Naan bread and four bottled waters for it to subside. I was ill for the rest of the night.

The next day, we hired a car to drive us to an important meeting, 90 minutes away. Our host was demanding, argumentative, and uncooperative, resulting in a complete waste of our time. Everything he had agreed to over the phone and via email during the proceeding weeks was now invalid, and in my mind, I concluded that our trip to Mumbai was a bust. My cortisol levels were pegged, and I was beyond done! It was time to find my gratitude.

That night, I put on some shorts, grabbed my headphones, and headed to the hotel pool. While lying in the cushioned lounger, I closed my eyes and listened to soft, relaxing music. I took slow, deep breaths and visualized all of the things about this trip that I loved. The kindness and hospitality of the people. The beauty and color of the culture. The delicious food (minus the pepper). If it was positive, I focused on it. Then I began to verbalize the things in my life that I was grateful for—my wife and kids, my friends, being paid to travel to other countries. Within 20 minutes I had taken control of my emotions, subdued my anxiety, and shifted my attitude to positive. By finding my gratitude, I had changed my mental state—as well as my experience.

Power Quote

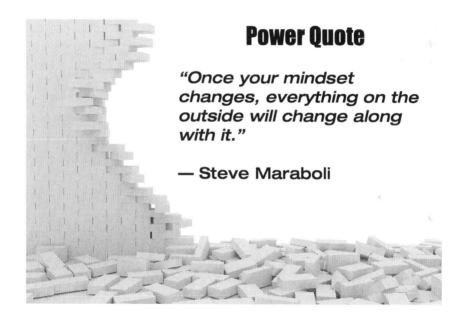

"Once your mindset changes, everything on the outside will change along with it."

— Steve Maraboli

35: EXPERTS GET INVOLVED

After finishing my time in the military, I moved back to Dayton for about a year, before getting a job with the airlines. I was dating a woman named Roxanne at the time, who had recently graduated from the University of Dayton. She had a larger-than-life personality and never turned a blind eye to an act of injustice. While driving one evening, I pulled over to get fuel. We were near a rough part of town, so we wanted to be quick about it—especially since the sun was going down.

As the car was fueling, we noticed a child frantically running through the parking lot. The girl had short brown hair and was completely naked, with tears streaming down her face. Trying to console her, we learned she had been kidnapped and was trying to escape from her captor, who was inside the store paying for his gas. The kidnapper had been driving on fumes and was forced to pull over, so he threatened the child with a large hunting knife if she tried to escape. With tremendous bravery, she made a run for it once he entered the store.

Without hesitation, Roxanne grabbed the 10-year-old child, wrapped a coat around her, and locked the two of them inside the car, while I stood guard. Aware of what was happening, the kidnapper bolted from the store. And, knowing there was no possible way he was getting the child back, he jumped in his vehicle and took off—squealing his tires as he headed into traffic. He looked like Charles Manson, with his crazy eyes, thick dark hair, and scraggly beard. At that moment, we had a crucial decision to make. Did we follow him in a high-speed car chase with hopes of getting his license plate number? Or, did we make the safe choice and call the police? Our biggest concern was that he would go free and target the girl again, or possibly others. The choice was obvious—we had to pursue. As we weaved through traffic, the girl begged us not to follow her captor, but we had to get his plates, and we did our best not to lose him.

He was in a white, '70s Ford Bronco and driving like a maniac. Jumping curbs, zigzagging, last-minute exits—he tried desperately to shake us. I'll never forget when Roxanne shouted: "GOT IT!" It was just seconds before the kidnapper made a dangerous, last-minute exit off the freeway that we couldn't react to in time. With his license plate number memorized, we drove directly to the police station and gave a full report. Officers were quickly dispatched to the address where the vehicle was registered, leading them straight to an old farmhouse. They found the suspect hiding in a closet, buried under a pile of dirty clothes, and cleanly shaved. He matched the description we gave in our report and was arrested immediately. His Bronco was filled with children's shoes and clothing—he had done this before.

Since we remained close to the investigation—through police lineups and court hearings—we learned he was a serial pedophile, linked to more than a dozen unsolved child abductions. He had grabbed the girl from her bike in broad daylight, in a town 45 minutes away, while her dad was mowing the grass at a close distance. But, thanks to a life sentence without parole, he would never do it again. Roxanne and I were later invited to an annual awards ceremony in Dayton, where we each received commendations from the Chief of Police on behalf of the city. We will forever remain grateful that we were in the right place at the right time, and that we decided to get involved!

Power Quote

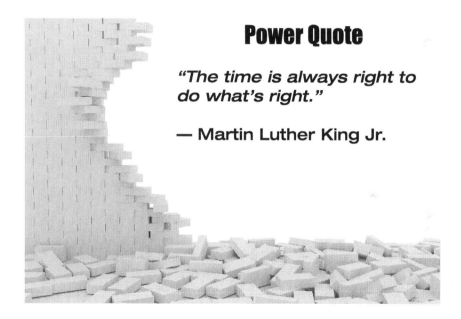

"The time is always right to do what's right."

— Martin Luther King Jr.

36: EXPERTS GO ALL IN

While serving in the United States Air Force as a young man, I began to dream for the first time in my life. My vision was to one day pursue a career in combatives training, but I had no idea where to begin. Anytime I wasn't on the flight line turning wrenches on a B-52 bomber, I was either taking martial arts lessons in town or teaching it on the base. At one point, while stationed in California, I was enrolled at three different schools at the same time (two as a student and one as an instructor). This proved to be the season of my life when I was laying low, getting strong, and finding myself.

Days before exiting the military, I took oral, written, and practical exams with the FAA to earn my Airframe and Powerplant licenses, with the goal of working for the airlines. Fast-forward a few years to 1992, and I was now living in Fort Worth, employed with American Airlines as an aircraft mechanic. I worked on Boeing 767s during the day and drove to Dallas in the evenings, where I was the hand-to-hand combat instructor for the National Bodyguard Association. On nights when I wasn't driving to Dallas, I was teaching private self-defense lessons in the living room of my apartment. On the weekends, I was improving my combatives skills by training at two different schools.

I had been going hard-core in the martial arts for several years by then, with the goal of creating a hybrid system that I could teach to law enforcement and the military—as a full-time career. In my heart, I was conflicted because I was trying to serve two masters at the same time. I was burned out, stressed out, and too indecisive to do anything about it. American Airlines was a solid company with great pay and benefits, and the thought of leaving seemed like insanity. If I followed my heart and crashed and burned in the process, there would be nobody standing in the shadows to rescue me. Furthermore, I had tasted the bitterness of poverty as a child, and my fear of loss was greater than my desire for gain.

Beyond frustrated, it was time to do a personal inventory and choose between job security or pursuing my passion, once and for all. I was quickly earning a good reputation in the combatives industry and had some strong connections from the military. I also had a handful of private students, was still training bodyguards on the side, and was providing executive protection to some high-end clients. The stage was set, and the conundrum was over—I was going all in!

I'll never forget the look on my manager's face when I told him my plans while turning in my two weeks' notice. He looked at me like I was out of my mind and repeatedly asked if I was sure. He reminded me of the hundreds of candidates who were on a waiting list for my job, meaning I couldn't come back if things didn't work out. Nonetheless, my mind was made up. Two weeks later I pushed all of my chips to the middle of the table, turned in my I.D. badge, loaded up my tools, and exited through the turnstile for the last time.

Over the next 12 months, I faced countless challenges and adversities. Money was scarce, and sleep was fleeting, but my sense of fulfillment was abundant. I took the risk to follow my dreams, and my life is better for it.

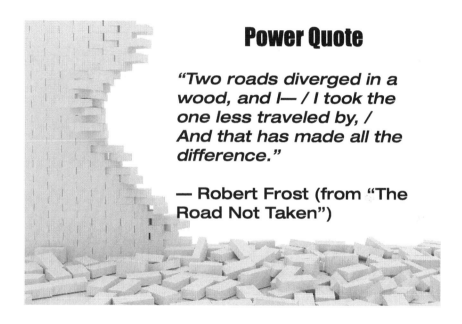

Power Quote

"Two roads diverged in a wood, and I— / I took the one less traveled by, / And that has made all the difference."

— Robert Frost (from "The Road Not Taken")

37: EXPERTS STAY GROUNDED

My decision in 1992 to walk away from a great career with American Airlines to start my own combatives business was a massive risk for me at the time. But, within a few years, this decision began to pay off, making the '90s a season of increase (or so I thought). I was beginning to earn a good name for myself, which led to referrals, which led to bigger jobs. I had a nice corner office overlooking the Dallas skyline, I had a steady stream of clients, and for the first time in my life, I had a little money. I was being paid $100 per hour for one-on-one private training, teaching pro athletes, entertainers, and executives alike. This was more than double what other martial arts instructors were charging at the time. As a personal safety expert, I was being interviewed on the news, invited as a guest on several talk shows, and I was featured in magazine and newspaper articles.

The Harris Self-Defense Team consisted of me and three phenomenal black belt instructors; we always moved as a unit when we conducted demos and training. These three men were highly gifted and talented athletes, who knew how to get a crowd on their feet—and keep them there. We were sponsored by a major sports clothing manufacturer, which provided us with more athletic attire than we knew what to do with, and we were thrilled. Depending on what events we had on the calendar, we would receive boxes of corresponding "theme-colored" team gear, so we could bear our sponsor's name in style, anytime we were in the spotlight. They sent us stars and stripes warm-up suits for our Fourth of July martial arts demonstration, where thousands were expected to attend. We received blue and white warm-ups for the Dallas Cowboys Super Bowl Parade, where we were providing team security for the players and the Vince Lombardi Trophy. I was invited to participate in celebrity charity events and VIP backroom parties, and I was loving all of the attention. The problem was, this new lifestyle was lacking the substance I was longing for, and I was beginning to lose my way.

Growing up, I always believed that money and fame would fix most of life's problems, but I was now getting a front-row seat to the lives of the rich and famous, and the majority of them seemed lost and empty. The pendulum of life had swung to the far left during my childhood, due to want and neglect. Now, just a little success was swinging the pendulum to the far right. I needed to find the middle—a place of peace and balance. Pleasure wears off in the morning, but joy hangs around long after the party is over. I wanted joy. I knew I had to get my head out of the clouds and become firmly grounded in something with true substance, something bigger than myself—but I didn't know how. I was ready to plant my feet on a foundation firmer than shifting sand, but what did that look like and where would I find it? I wanted to look in the mirror and love what I saw, which was the best version of myself. My search for purpose and significance had officially begun.

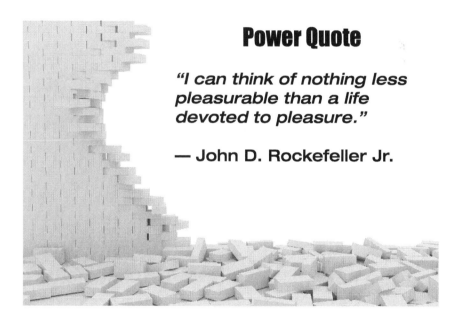

Power Quote

"I can think of nothing less pleasurable than a life devoted to pleasure."

— John D. Rockefeller Jr.

38: EXPERTS FIND THEIR DASH

I remember the first time I heard the famous line spoken by Mel Gibson in the movie *Braveheart*, back in 1995, when he so passionately said: "Every man dies. Not every many truly lives." Those powerful words stirred my soul deeply, most likely due to the life-changing epiphany that I had experienced just one year earlier. Let me explain. I was working late at my office one evening and stood up from my desk to stretch my legs. I looked through the large plate glass window of my top-floor corner office, taking in the well-lit Dallas skyline, when all of a sudden I became overwhelmed with a feeling of emptiness. At that moment, I remember saying to myself, "Chris, snap out of it!" These feelings were ambushing me from left field and made no sense whatsoever. I had a career that I loved and provided me with a good income, lots of friends, and I was in great health. So where was this coming from, and why now?

For the next few hours, all alone in my office, I took an honest inventory of my life while staring through the lens of personal conviction—and I was not happy with what I saw. Final analysis: It was on that night that I came to the sober realization that my feeling of emptiness was the result of living a life that had become all about me. In short, I was only living for myself. This was the night that I found my dash.

Engraved on most tombstones are the date of our birth and the date of our death, with a small dash in between. Through much introspection, I have learned that the dash in the middle is significantly more important than the numbers themselves. For some people, merely surviving until death is their dash, with self-preservation being their ultimate driver. For others, the dash may be their success, their career, their family, or a worthwhile cause. But for me, thanks to that hot summer night in Texas, I can sum up my dash with one simple sentence: "The success that I want for myself, I want for everyone."

Knowing what you want to be known for and how you want to be remembered after you're gone can have a significant impact on your life, as well as the lives of others. However, if you're unable to articulate these answers, it may be simpler to begin by declaring how you *don't* want to be remembered. The good news is, if you don't like the answer you're faced with, you might not have to change what you're currently doing. Instead, you may just need to change the motives behind why you're doing it. Either way, by discovering these answers now, you will create a three-dimensional road map that can lead you to a more fulfilled life. A life that's brilliantly colored with your core values and brimming with a sense of purpose. Now, go find your dash!

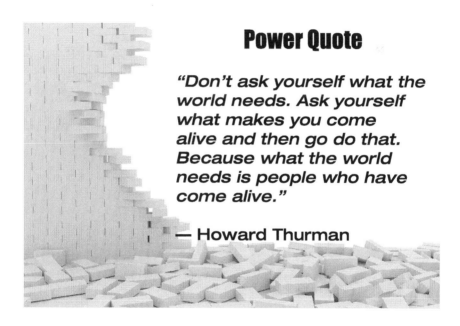

Power Quote

"Don't ask yourself what the world needs. Ask yourself what makes you come alive and then go do that. Because what the world needs is people who have come alive."

— Howard Thurman

39: EXPERTS SHARE THEIR POWER

My heroes are not the people I admire and respect the most. Instead, they are those kind and thoughtful souls who believed in me when nobody else did—perhaps not even myself. I will never forget those who have inspired me, encouraged me, and challenged me along my journey. I hope that I always continue to pay it forward by sharing the expert power I've gained along the way with those who need it most—just like I needed it.

Some of my mentors have poured into my life, others have sprinkled me just at the right time, and there are those who doused me with a bucket of cold water when I couldn't get out of my own way. Then, there are those, whom I've never met, who have invested in my life—like Zig Ziglar and Napoleon Hill, just to name a few. A great deal of what I know about selling with integrity and purpose I learned through Zig Ziglar's books, and Napoleon Hill taught me the significance of having a positive mental attitude, with words that he penned more than 80 years ago. Who believed in you the most? Who has mentored you? Who has shared their expert power with you?

Across the street from my high school was an old white farmhouse that sat on several acres of land, with a small building the size of a two-car garage positioned off to the side. Frank Grant, an internationally recognized martial arts expert, lived there. He had converted the small building into a dojo to teach Okinawan Shorin-Ryu three times a week. Although his rates were very reasonable at $35 per month in 1982, I didn't have the money. But I desperately wanted to learn from this incredible man. Through his kindness, he agreed to let me (a clueless 15-year-old boy) work off my monthly dues by doing trivial things, such as arriving to class early and cleaning the dojo, paying meticulous attention to the hardwood floors. In 2012, some 30 years later, I sent him a heartfelt email, not knowing if he would ever receive it, let alone remember me. In my email, I expressed my sincere gratitude for the life-changing impact he had on me as a boy and how I had made martial arts my profession, thanks in part to his positive influence on my life. To my surprise, I got a response. Remaining true to form, he stated that he was proud to be instrumental in my journey, followed by a few other encouraging remarks that I have locked away in my heart.

As an adult, I am always on the lookout for mentors and mentees, as I firmly believe we need both to maintain a healthy equilibrium between our spirit, soul, and body. The primary quality I look for in a mentor is their mastery of the subject that I am seeking to develop further in myself. In other words, if my goal is to become more fit, I will seek someone who is fit (and had to work to obtain it). And, when it comes to mentoring someone, I prefer to invest my time in those who are teachable, have a positive attitude, are grateful, and who are ready to do the work. I believe that sharing the power we accumulate on our journey is a key component to creating a fulfilling life. It is our contribution to others that puts steam in our stride and purpose in our hearts. Experience has taught me that by sharing my power I will always have more.

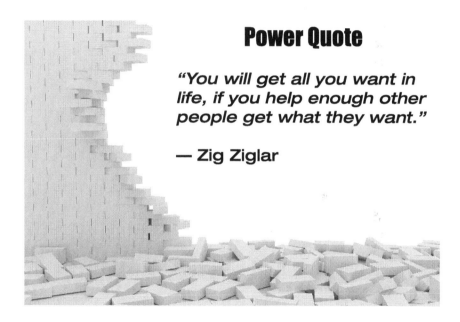

Power Quote

"You will get all you want in life, if you help enough other people get what they want."

— Zig Ziglar

40: EXPERTS FINISH THE JOB

In 2011 I was invited to Madrid, Spain, by my new European sponsor to do a whirlwind training tour. The purpose of the trip would be twofold: I would showcase my skills as a master combatives instructor and demonstrate a nonlethal law enforcement device I had invented and patented, which my sponsor would be selling as my distributor. I was eager for my invention to get a fair evaluation by the law enforcement and military community in Europe, but I was equally excited about the high-level combatives training I would be conducting.

I arrived over the weekend but would teach from Monday through Friday, with two training sessions per day, each four hours long, and at different locations. That meant I would be teaching 10 physically demanding classes in just five days, each one to highly trained and seasoned professionals. This ambitious regimen consisted of training law enforcement, SWAT, and military instructors, and our schedule did not allow for delays. My new sponsor had put his name and reputation on the line with his customers, and I gave my word that I was up for the task.

During the first training session on the first day, I was throwing a flurry of punches at a military soldier to validate that the block I had just taught the class would now be an automatic, instinctive reaction. While throwing the final hook, I heard a loud popping sound come from my right side. I had just torn my tricep muscle, and I knew it. On the airplane ride over, I kept reminding myself: budget your energy, pace yourself, be smart. Once there, however, I got caught up in the energy of the room and my well-rehearsed game plan went right out the window—and on the first day! I was in excruciating pain as the next participant hurried to the line to showcase his ability. He gave me the nod, affirming that he was ready to be attacked, so I soldiered on while trying to conceal my grimace.

Each class I taught, each student I faced, the tear worsened. All I could think about was how this family-owned distributorship had put 30 years of their professional relationships on the line to make this week happen, and I wasn't about to make them regret it. I just had to make it to Friday at 6 p.m., no matter what! Javier was the son of the company's founder and was assigned to be my interpreter and driver throughout the week. He had a tremendous work ethic, a positive mental attitude, and was strong in character. He knew something was wrong and kept asking me, in English and off to the side: "Are you OK, sir?" It was obvious something was amiss, but he understood how important it was that we continue. Javier's father had devoted his life to building a strong reputation in the law enforcement and military community—canceling a week of events at the last minute was not an option.

Painstakingly, we made it through the week while I taught hundreds of professionals, without a single delay, cancellation, or excuse. Each group and organization that participated was extremely pleased, new relationships were forged, and I learned a great deal about myself in the process. Although the itinerary I signed up for was grossly unrealistic (my eyes were bigger than my stomach), I completed the week with a sense of pride and accomplishment because I stayed the course, kept my word, and finished the job.

Power Quote

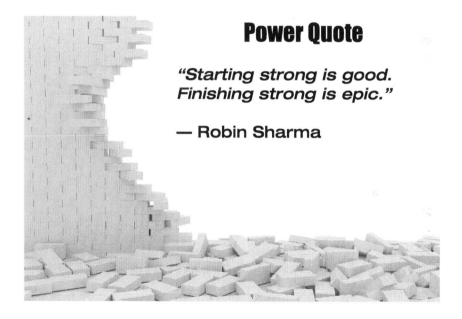

*"Starting strong is good.
Finishing strong is epic."*

— Robin Sharma

41: EXPERTS CREATE A PLAN

I am a strong advocate of hope and the power of positive thinking, but as the saying goes: Hope is not a strategy. If you're going to advance in life, you need to create a road map, and it's vital that you follow it. Success doesn't just happen by accident—it has to be planned. I believe in setting goals so big that we have to grow into them—but do it in phases and definitely on purpose. Years ago, I created a seven-step action plan for how to systematically achieve my personal and professional goals. Over the years, I've shared this strategy with countless others whose lives are a testament to its effectiveness. It's tried, it's proven, and when properly applied—it works! Here are the seven steps:

One: Determine Exactly What You Want

The first step is to write down your desired goals, using specific details that can be accurately measured. For example, don't say something like "I want to lose weight" or "I want to lose 20 pounds." Instead, state something like "I will weigh this much by this date." Remember that when it comes to setting goals, if it can't be measured, it doesn't exist.

Two: Decide That You Are Deserving of It

Earl Nightingale is quoted as having said: "Whatever we plant in our subconscious mind and nourish with repetition and emotion will one day become a reality." The subconscious mind is a powerful force, and whether you think you can or think you can't, you'll most likely be right in the end. Doubt has killed more dreams than failure ever has, so before targeting a goal, it's crucial that we get our mindset right.

Three: Commit to Not Quitting Until It's Yours

Tenacity is one's ability to forge ahead when tempted to quit. Anytime you feel like giving up, focus on why you started in the first place. The discomfort of pushing through is a temporary thing—

but stopping short of the finish line can be far more painful and long-lasting. Before you begin, commit that you will see it to the end—regardless. Don't give in, never give up, and give it all you've got—you're worth it!

Four: Create a Daily Action Plan and Start Today

A daily action plan is a simple list of new habits, standards, or self-imposed rules that one is committed to following. It's the consistency and accumulation of these small stepping stones that eventually leads us toward the realization of obtaining what we want. There's never a perfect time to begin doing the work, so start right where you are—today! A month from now you'll be glad you did.

Five: Eliminate Distractions and Protect Your Assets

Most people are keenly aware of what their biggest distractions are—the challenge is exercising the self-discipline required to remove them. Goals and distractions can rarely coexist, so when you're ready to get serious, kick your distractions to the curb. Your three greatest assets are your time, your energy, and your mindset—protect them! How well you protect these assets will determine your success.

Six: When You Fall, Get Up—Again and Again

The road that leads to a worthwhile goal is often littered with potholes, speed bumps, and obstacles. When pursuing our goals, we are highly susceptible to exhaustion, discouragement, and mistakes. Expect some bumps, bruises, and temporary setbacks along the way—it's part of the journey. And when you fall, get up, dust yourself off, and move on down the road. Falling is natural—but try to fall forward.

Seven: With Gratitude and Integrity—Do the Work

Nothing is a substitute for gratitude, integrity, and hard work. When these three things are combined for a common purpose, our determination becomes an unstoppable force, and our destination becomes an immovable object. Remain grateful, walk upright, and put in the effort—then watch the transformation.

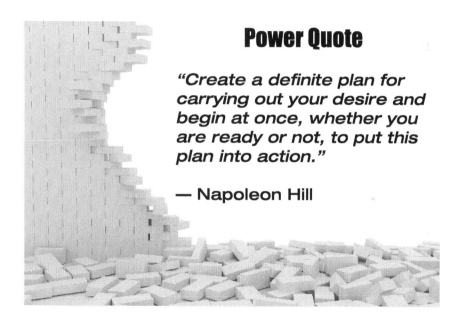

Power Quote

"Create a definite plan for carrying out your desire and begin at once, whether you are ready or not, to put this plan into action."

— Napoleon Hill

42: EXPERTS IMMERSE

In the 1953 Warner Bros. movie *Hondo,* a cavalryman named Lane (played by John Wayne) picks up a six-year-old boy, Johnny, and throws him into the water—as his way of teaching the boy how to swim. Wildly flailing his arms in the middle of the stream, Johnny frantically struggles to stay afloat. But he eventually begins to paddle and swims safely to the other side. Johnny had just been exposed to an extreme form of immersion training—literally! When I make a firm decision to achieve a new goal or earn a new expert power, I fully immerse myself into its attainment, eliminating all distractions and becoming laser focused on the end result. Learning how to completely submerge yourself into something, with firm guidelines and deadlines set in place, is an invaluable skill set to possess.

Once a goal has been set, how do I immerse myself in achieving it? The first thing I do is allocate the time that will be required—in advance. I then practice time blocking by assigning specific tasks that must be completed during each session. Since my success is dependent on my ability to protect this time, I have to be comfortable saying "NO" to myself and others—and often! During my "all-in" phase, I typically wake up at 3 a.m. every morning, brush my teeth, make a pot of coffee, and get to work. This means my evenings are usually cut short—since I have to go to bed early. But I don't mind, because "what I want most is stronger than what I want now!" Having a few extra distraction-free hours each day excels my productivity to a whole new level—it's truly a game changer. And, since most sane people are still sleeping, I'm not stealing from that part of my day where I need to be focused on producing cash flow—or spending time with my family. Also, I normally go to the gym six days per week, but when submerged, I reduce my workouts to three days per week—survival mode is efficient.

The second thing I do is eliminate all possible distractions, especially the negative ones. When I need to hunker down, television time is the first item to get cut. I then let my friends know that I'm about to go off the grid, and for how long, so they understand why I can't come out and play—clear and open communication is the key. For entertainment, I switch to my "inspirational music playlist," which is comprised exclusively of positive and encouraging songs that help keep me motivated. This is the only type of music I listen to when I'm in the arena with resistance staring me down. If it's negative, it goes! I stay close to my encouragers and supporters, and distance myself from the energy hogs.

The third and final thing I do is set a nonnegotiable deadline for crossing the finish line—with mini checkpoints along the way. Identifying a hard stop is crucial due to the high level of intensity, self-discipline, and personal sacrifice that's required. I can endure a great deal of discomfort, deprivation, and delayed gratification—but only if there's a clear end in sight. I can only run full speed for so long, and when I'm sprinting, I have to see the finish line.

After much deliberation, once I finally settled on the direction I wanted to go with this book, I gave myself 100 days to write it—from start to finish. This firm deadline has kept me from straying off task on countless occasions. Also, I always keep sight of the fact that my "full-throttle" commitments will tip the scales of my work-life balance—so I always get buy-in from my inner circle, especially from those who will be missing my companionship or picking up my slack. The effectiveness of "goal immersion" is tied to the fact that it's a temporary thing, so get in, grab the dream, and get out—no messing around! So, what's that thing you really want: a bigger paycheck, a healthier body, to write a book? I've just shared with you my secret recipe for attainment—but action is the yeast that makes it rise. You will be surprised how much you can endure, if you want something badly enough. Self-discipline and personal sacrifice are the currency that pays for your dreams—all you have to do is earn it. You are capable of far more than you know.

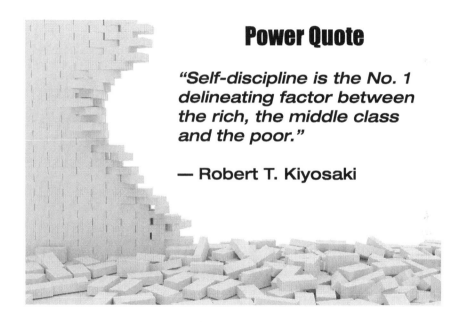

Power Quote

"Self-discipline is the No. 1 delineating factor between the rich, the middle class and the poor."

— Robert T. Kiyosaki

43: EXPERTS ARE UPSTANDERS

In 1991 I was living in Tulsa, Oklahoma, and working for American Airlines. Sometimes, after work, I would go to my favorite burger joint, which was within a stone's throw of my apartment. The owner of the grill, whom I will call Ray, to respect his privacy, was a kind and gentle soul. He was in his mid-40s, had salt-and-pepper hair, and was always smiling. He had an '80s Wurlitzer jukebox, several dartboards, and he always served his steady stream of regulars generous portions. It was a family-friendly atmosphere, where everyone knew your name and you were acknowledged with enthusiasm when you walked through the door.

One evening, I arrived at the grill after a hard day's work and was surprised to see a large group of people gathered in the parking lot. I got out of my Mercury Cougar and approached the crowd to see what all the commotion was about. After pushing my way through, I could see it was a one-sided fight. A very large man in his late 20s had Ray, the owner, in a standing headlock and was hitting him repeatedly. Making a quick scan of the crowd, I was shocked to see I was standing next to many of the regulars. Why were they just standing there? Why weren't they helping our friend?

Shouting "enough," I charged this "mountain of a man" and quickly pulled him off my friend by applying agitated pressure to his septum with my index finger, forcing him to release his victim. I then remained in front of the aggressor until the police arrived, countering multiple attempts to hurt my friend further. I would later learn that the man had been released from prison just a few days earlier. Now, angry at life, he walked into the grill and began harassing the patrons and the staff. When Ray confronted him and asked the man to leave, the ex-convict dragged him to the parking lot to teach him a lesson and to vent his frustrations. The sad part is, lots of regular customers followed closely behind. None to help. All to watch. During my time living in the projects as a child, I was the one lying in the center of the circle, curled in the fetal position—surrounded by an audience that refused to help. It was because of these firsthand experiences that I adopted mottos like: "Protect the innocent and safeguard the helpless." And "If not me, then who?" And "If not now, then when?" It was those life events that strengthened my resolve to not be indifferent and to offer my assistance to those in need, when able.

Many years have passed since that evening, but I'm still no closer to understanding how so many stood silently on the sidelines and remained indifferent as our friend was being physically hurt. I understand that most people could not have stood up to the ex-con's size and temper without putting themselves in great danger. I can also make allowances for those who were in shock and frozen with indecision. But the others who safely watched from the sidelines while doing nothing at all? Call 911 or yell at the top of your lungs—just do something! You don't have to be a hero, just don't be a spectator. Today, there are those who record heinous acts with their smartphones for evidentiary purposes. Then, there are those who record heinous acts to get likes and views on social media. The first, I applaud. The second, I abhor. A bystander is someone who is present at an event but chooses not to intervene. An upstander, however, is someone who intervenes by doing what they can—no matter how small. My heroes of today are the upstanders—and I choose to be one.

Power Quote

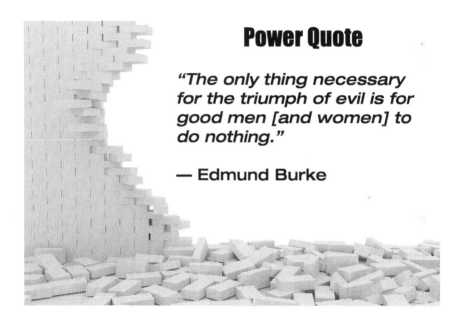

"The only thing necessary for the triumph of evil is for good men [and women] to do nothing."

— Edmund Burke

44: EXPERTS PERSEVERE

Is there something you started in your past but didn't finish? Something that you find yourself thinking about—all the time? You know, that one unfinished chapter of your life that you would love to go back and close, but don't know how? If so, this story is for you!

After completing our work in Central America, my wife, Corrie, decided she wanted to go back to college and finish earning her degree. She had completed just one year when she was 19 years old, and it had always gnawed at her that she stopped short of the goal. She had dropped out after her first year because she couldn't silence the voice of a former high school teacher who told her: "College isn't for you, dear. Marry well." Corrie was now ready to confront this ugly lie and fight this fire-breathing dragon from her past—head on!

Because our kids were nine and 11 years old, they were able to do a lot for themselves, and the time seemed right to begin this long journey. So, in the fall of 2009, Corrie enrolled at Collin County Community College and began her academic climb. In her mid-30s at the time, Corrie found herself immersed in an environment and culture that was dominated by students who were 15 years her junior. There were generational gaps between Corrie and her classmates, and many of her professors were her age. This made communication sometimes interesting, if not challenging. But, remaining true to form, she always adapted and overcame—and built relationships along the way. Before she knew it, she was walking down the aisle, wearing her blue cap and gown, and displaying the awards she had earned. After two years of hard work and sacrifice, she was awarded her associate degree, graduating magna cum laude. She only knows one way to do things, which is with excellence.

Because of her award-winning academic performance during her time at the community college, Corrie earned a Presidential Scholarship to the University of Texas at Arlington. Without delay and with a new target in sight, she grabbed the next rung of the ladder and began to climb higher. The courses were harder and the study requirements were intense, yet she persevered. Within two years she walked the aisle, receiving her honors bachelor's degree, and once again she finished magna cum laude. Having sufficiently "untied the lie" from her high school teacher and determining that college was for her, she lost no momentum and set her sights on a master's degree at Southern Methodist University (SMU).

Working full time and pursuing her master's degree, Corrie faced new levels of difficulty and intensity. She was raising two teenagers and volunteering at their school, and helping manage our combatives training business while I traveled internationally. Juggling these responsibilities while pursuing her master's proved to be significantly more challenging than when she juggled them during her undergrad studies, but yet she persisted. I'm proud to say that Corrie graduated magna cum laude again and is now working on her second master's, an MBA from Cox School of Business—where she will undoubtedly finish strong. She has learned that greatness lives on the other side of inconvenience, and it's because of Corrie's inner strength, persistence, and willingness to pay the price that she continues to go thru! What lies from your past are holding you back? Are you ready to confront them and climb to new heights?

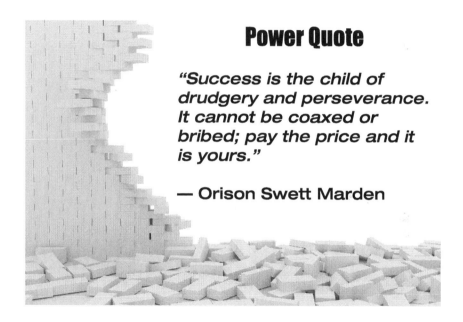

Power Quote

"Success is the child of drudgery and perseverance. It cannot be coaxed or bribed; pay the price and it is yours."

— Orison Swett Marden

45: EXPERTS LEVERAGE EXPERTS

When my son was nine, and we were living in Central America, he told me he wanted to learn boxing. After asking more than a dozen locals where we should train, they all pointed me to the same man. When my son and I arrived at our first class, we realized that the "outdoor boxing school" was directly on top of a trash heap, partially covered with dirt. We were each handed broken extension cords but had no idea why. After being scolded by our coach for just standing there, we learned that these cords were our jump ropes and it was time to start jumping! Homemade heavy bags, filled with sawdust, hung from old swing sets. And if you wanted to lift weights, not a problem—there were lots of large automotive parts laying around—like a car axle for bicep curls! The cardio area was a row of old semitruck tires laying on their sides. When you sprint in place while standing on a 22-inch truck tire, your balance gets a free tune-up while your thighs cramp and burn like crazy! Oh, and the students chased chickens—just like in the movie *Rocky*. My favorite part was when we trained in the rain and the smell of our trash heap became putrid—but nobody seemed to mind. After our first class, on our way home, my son asked, "Why are we training at this place, Dad?" I looked at him and said, "Because this is where the top expert in the city is, and to become the best, you have to work with the best." I could see in my son's eyes that he got it. We trained there for the next several months—he never complained.

Countless times during my life I've been asked, "Who taught you martial arts?" My answer has always been the same: Lots of different experts from lots of different places. You don't get hired to train the pros unless you're one yourself—and turning pro takes a great deal more than watching how-to videos and reading books. You've got to find the best in their field and pursue them as closely as they will allow—with ears and eyes wide open. I learned Muay Thai in Oklahoma, Kung Fu in

California, aikido in Texas, and boxing in Missouri. Anytime I moved to a new city, my first priority was always to find the top martial arts instructor around and begin training with him or her immediately. And, I never squawked about their rates or their availability. Experience has taught me that when we want something badly enough, we make the time and we find the money—which is exactly what I did. Don't get me wrong, I've got lots of interesting scars from the times I went the cheap route—thinking I was the smartest guy in the room because I hired the lowest bidder—those lessons hurt! Life has taught me that when it comes to leveraging experts, experience and quality are priceless!

When I decided to write this book and improve my presentation skills, I hired Christy Kercheville from Pinnacle You to mentor me on this important journey. Were her rates the lowest? *Nope.* Was her customized training program easy? *Not even close.* Did she require me to do the work? *Darn straight!* And, did her professional coaching make me and *I Go Thru* significantly better? *Absolutely!* Her terms were simple: I paid the price and put in the hours, and she transferred countless years of experience into my personal success and development. I also leveraged the talent of a few carefully selected personal relationships for this project, like Roy and Diane Mitchell of Mitchell Thompson Interiors. As luxury interior designers, Roy and Diane have an exceptional eye for detail and always strive for excellence. Reviewing the chapters as they were written, they continuously spotted the "little things" that were big in impact and would have otherwise been missed. Experts surround us, but we have to find them, pursue them, and listen to them. Aligning ourselves and our projects with the right professionals can be worth its weight in gold. What one person can transfer in the form of knowledge, experience, and wisdom can save years of precious time and produce a lifetime of dividends. So, when it comes to the important stuff, never skimp on talent. Instead, insist on only hiring the best.

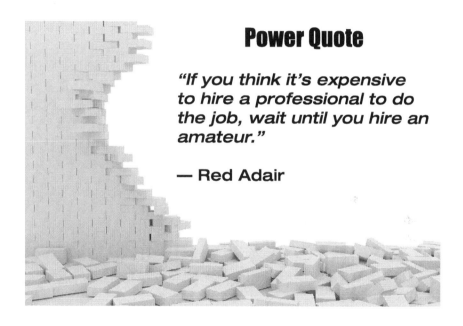

Power Quote

"If you think it's expensive to hire a professional to do the job, wait until you hire an amateur."

— Red Adair

190

46: EXPERTS DELEGATE

In 1998 I was personally invited to visit the Arab Gulf States region to conduct demonstrations for three U.S. allied countries. The objective was simple: I was there to secure new contracts for myself and my sponsor. Since each demo would be given at full speed and with full intensity, Sean Henchey joined me on the journey. Sean was one of my full-time employees, and he was an exceptional fighter—lightning fast and tough as nails. For our first round of events, we traveled to Kuwait. From there, we flew 360 miles to Qatar (currently, Qatar hosts the largest U.S. military base in the Middle East). We then proceeded to the United Arab Emirates, where we conducted demos in both Abu Dhabi and Dubai. We were to prove our skill set to generals, ambassadors, and special forces. Play fighting or choreographed fight scenes would offend our audience and get us sent home immediately. It was time to put up or shut up.

Although exhausting, the trip was a huge success and landed me the largest training contract of my career, at the time. I agreed to provide my signature combatives training to military and special forces personnel in Qatar. To complete the contract, it would take two black belt instructors eight consecutive weeks, working full time. And, as badly as I wanted to do the job myself, it would have put my growing business in jeopardy if I left the U.S. for two full months. I was already spinning too many plates. This was an important contract that could lead to a lot more work in the region, as well as the U.S., and the thought of not handling it myself made me nervous. But my business had hit its tipping point. I either scaled back my customers in the States and packed my bags for Qatar, or I would have to delegate the job to experts I had trained well—allowing me to remain in Dallas while taking my business to the next level.

Floyd Powell was the total package when it came to black belts. Whatever he put his hands to, he did with all his might—

and he didn't know the word quit. As a former wrestler, he was a perfectionist when it came to technique, and he had loads of natural ability. My decision was made—it was time to trust. Floyd and Sean would make the trip on my behalf—the future of my business was in their hands.

Each day, Floyd and Sean were woken abruptly by the 5 a.m. morning prayer, which was broadcasted through a loudspeaker. They would then shower, eat breakfast, and await their assigned driver, who would take them to the military base. Their days were long, intense, and very physical. Training hundreds of soldiers, ranging from infantry level to special forces, they put their shoulders to the plow, each and every day. Admittedly, delegating such an important assignment to these two professionals seemed like a big risk in the beginning, but I soon viewed their value in an entirely different light.

Through weekly correspondence, I learned how well Floyd and Sean were respected by our hosts. Military generals as well as members of the Qatari royal family had come to trust my representatives at a deep level. These high-ranking officials took my instructors four-wheeling in the desert, falcon hunting on their estates, and gave them tours of their nostalgic birthplaces. By choosing to delegate to these proven and trustworthy professionals, both my business and brand were expanded and experienced new heights. We can move mountains when we properly leverage the power of the right people.

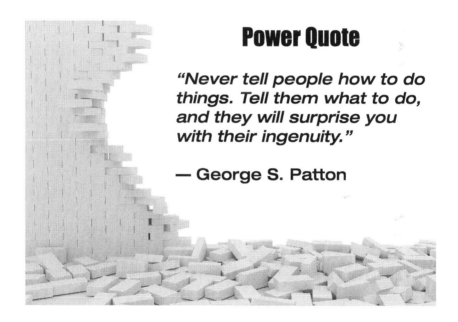

Power Quote

"Never tell people how to do things. Tell them what to do, and they will surprise you with their ingenuity."

— George S. Patton

47: EXPERTS STEP UP

Adjacent to the orphanage my wife and I ran in Nicaragua was the small town of Chilamatillo. This tight-knit community was laid out in a grid pattern, with numerous dirt roads pointing in all four directions. These signless streets were peppered with large potholes and lined with shanties on both sides, which housed nearly 800 people. And, although some of these structures were constructed of bricks or cinder blocks (usually the churches), most were nothing more than dilapidated shacks. These humble shelters had dirt floors, no plumbing, and were held together with sheets of rusted corrugated steel, plywood, and plastic tarps. If it could be salvaged, hauled, and tied down, they could build a home with it.

Chilamatillo had one well, which was powered by an old electric pump that was buried deep underground. Positioned in the center of town, this well was a major life source for the community—providing all of their water for cooking, cleaning, hygiene, and drinking. Every day, someone from each home would journey to the well while carrying as many containers as possible. Electricity for the pump traveled across sagging, overhanging power lines, and was provided by the Spanish electric company, Unión Fenosa. At the end of each month, the town received one utility bill, which was divided equally amongst each home. A man who lived in the community would go door to door, showing the bill and collecting the cash. If you didn't pay, you didn't get water—so everyone paid.

One day, a group of four men entered the town, each ranged from 30 to 40 years of age. They had decided to target Chilamatillo for monthly extortion and began showing up on the same day as the town collections—clearly there was an insider. They took the money that had been collected, by force, if necessary. These men always traveled together, with two of them holstering machetes by their sides—this was not their only town. This resulted in the bill not being paid, electricity being turned off, and the town going without water. On countless occasions, the orphanage would provide water to Chilamatillo by filling a 500-gallon tank from our well and pulling it with our tractor. Anytime our tractor entered the town, the people would come running with buckets in hand, forming a line at the dysfunctional well.

Church pastors and leaders from the town requested a meeting with me and asked if I would help. I gladly paid the Unión Fenosa bill, and the electricity was restored. But, since the pump was old, being shut off had caused it to seize up permanently, and it now had to be replaced, which was going to cost $3,500. This time, the town leaders pleaded for my help. I agreed to raise the money from American donors under one condition—the thugs had to go! The leaders had already reported the extortion to the local police, but it hadn't helped. And, I was not about to raise money for a new pump, only to see it sit idle because the money was being stolen by a band of thieves. The solution was obvious: I would have to step up and deal with it myself.

Learning their routine, I met the four thieves at the time and place of my choosing, when they least expected it. I wielded a baseball bat and was not intimidated by their numbers, threats, or machetes. Since I'm not an advocate of vigilante justice, I'll skip the details. However, on that hot summer night, we came to an understanding and the issue was resolved, once and for all. The new pump was purchased, the water was restored, and the thugs never bothered the people of Chilamatillo again.

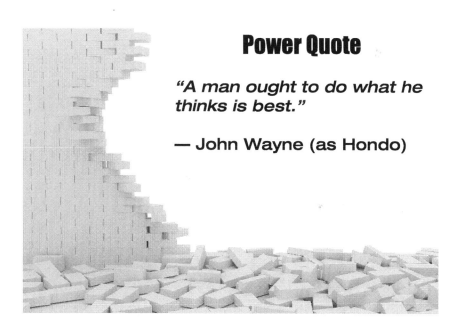

Power Quote

"A man ought to do what he thinks is best."

— John Wayne (as Hondo)

48: EXPERTS START OVER

Approximately five years ago, I was working in Dammam, Saudi Arabia, while fulfilling a contract between my Saudi sponsor and me. Dammam is a coastal city that rests on the Persian Gulf, and I lived within walking distance of the Dammam-Bahrain bridge, which is a 15-mile causeway that connects Saudi Arabia to the country of Bahrain. This engineering marvel is a sight to behold. I had signed a contract to work in the country for 10 weeks, with another 10-week extension guaranteed, if I chose to stay longer. Six weeks after arriving, my sponsor offered me an attractive two-year contract.

I lived in an elaborate, fully furnished villa that had five bathrooms and 10 sofas throughout the various rooms. It was adjacent to a mosque, which had a loudspeaker mounted at the top of a pole that would blast the morning prayer at 4 a.m., directly outside my bedroom window. I was provided a full-time assistant, who lived in the servant's quarters on the first floor, and we had the entire villa to ourselves. Aside from the master bedroom, where I chose to set up camp, and the large white kitchen, I never used the other rooms. And, because of the strict censorship of media and the internet, there was no entertainment and zero distractions, which gave me lots of alone time in the evenings.

I was assigned a full-time driver from India, who was also my interpreter. He spoke broken English, and it took a great deal of effort to understand one another, but we worked with what we had. Once, I was teaching close quarters combat to a group of 30 soldiers on a military base, when I saw my interpreter taking pictures of the training with his cell phone, which was strictly forbidden. When an officer harshly confronted him, he apologetically explained how he had interpreted "grab some bottled waters" as "take lots of photos." And, although he got off with a warning, he was required to spend the rest of the day sitting in the hot car.

For 10 weeks I worked until 5 p.m., had a workout at the gym or run along the beach, then I'd eat dinner, and then sit in my room and reflect—without distractions. I thought about all that I had missed with my children over the years while living on the road. I missed their first words, first steps, and first tooth. Hockey games, cheerleading practice, parent-teacher meetings—I had missed so much. And now, at 13 and 15, they were teenagers, who needed me more than ever. I had always justified my travel with: "I'm trying to give my children a better life than I had." But the truth was, if given a choice, my wife and kids would gladly have downsized our lifestyle, if it meant spending more time together.

After completing the first 10 weeks, I was given a two-week furlough, which I used to see my family. When I landed at the airport, I was met by my wife, who was ecstatic to see me and eager to talk. While nearly 8,000 miles apart, she and I had come to the same conclusion. Put simply, I couldn't be a road warrior during our children's teenaged years. My wife had always supported my career and was very proud of what I did, but it was time to find something that kept me close to home, at least until the kids graduated from high school. The problem was, I loved my career and couldn't imagine doing anything else. And, the thought of starting over in my 40s scared me. But my family came first, and I had to make a change. I graciously declined to extend my contract and never returned to Saudi Arabia. It was time to start the next chapter of my life, which would prove to be very fulfilling!

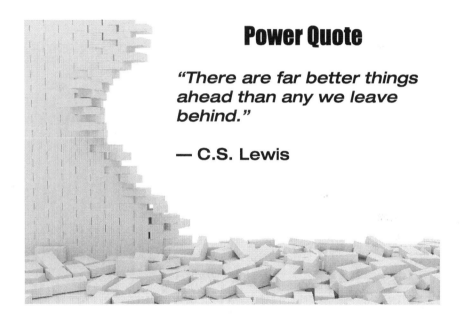

Power Quote

"There are far better things ahead than any we leave behind."

— C.S. Lewis

49: EXPERTS FIND THEIR PASSION

After arriving home from working a 10-week contract in Saudi Arabia, it was time to make a career change. I had to find something that would keep me in the Dallas area until my two teenagers graduated from high school. I had spent entirely too many nights away from them over the years, and I wanted to make this important season of their life my highest priority. The only problem was, I had no idea what I *wanted* to do. In the past, I had tried several things to supplement my income when the combatives business was slow or when I couldn't teach because I was healing from an injury. But this time was different. I was hanging up my black belt and starting a new career—from scratch. I always taught private lessons on the side, but that wasn't enough to support a family of four. It was time to update my résumé and start knocking on doors. I needed to find a job that kept me off the road and close to home.

Within three days of searching, I was hired to sell office copiers for a multinational technology company with more than 40,000 employees. It was a full-time position with a base salary, commissions, and good benefits. I would have to wear a tie and jacket every day and work from a small cubicle with walls so short everyone could see each other's face when seated. It was a competitive industry with a high turnover rate, and to keep my job I had to start selling—and keep selling.

This was a very depressing time for me. I had given up a career that I loved and exchanged it for a weekly paycheck. My success and achievements during my combatives career were due in part to my love of the craft and the knowledge that I was making a difference—maybe even saving lives. Starting over in my mid-40s and selling a product I was not passionate about was causing me to feel sorry for myself, as I struggled to find my sense of purpose. Self-pity can be a vicious opponent, and I was allowing it to beat me senseless.

I frequently reflected on my glory days, and my pride was getting the best of me; sometimes I lacked the motivation to get out of bed in the mornings. I needed to snap out it, find my gratitude, and change my attitude. I would remind myself of my responsibilities as a father, husband, and provider. This wasn't about me, and it wasn't about copiers. It was about doing what was best for my family. I had to find a way to get over myself and get back in the game.

A few months into my new job, I stepped off the elevator and was heading to my desk when I saw a large machine being installed in our demo room. It definitely wasn't a copier. When I asked the service technician about the machine, he handed me a 4-inch model of a shoe and said: "It prints parts like this. It's a 3-D printer. We're selling these now!" Looking at the colorful shoe, I could hardly believe my eyes. I hurried to my desk and began searching the internet, devouring information about 3-D printing. The more I learned, the more I wanted to know. This amazing technology was disrupting nearly every major industry in the world, and I wanted to be part of it. Suddenly, from one unexpected spark, I had found my passion again. My mind was made up—I was going to make a difference by selling 3-D printers, and I was going to be great at it—which is exactly what I did!

Power Quote

"Life is one big transition."

— Willie Stargell

50: EXPERTS TAKE OWNERSHIP

In 2015 I began a new career selling Additive Manufacturing Technology, otherwise known as 3-D printers. I was grateful for my new job and eager to get to work. There was just one problem—I didn't know anything about 3-D printers! I'll never forget my first day on the job, trying to get comfortable in my newly assigned cubicle as a six-foot-three, 250-pound weightlifter. As I continually bumped my knee into the filing cabinet, I recalled the scene in the movie *The Incredibles* where Bob Parr, an oversize claims adjuster, was maneuvering in his cubicle at Insuracare. This imagery helped me relax with a much-needed laugh.

Before I accepted my new job, I had spent the several months prior selling copiers for a multinational technology company with more than 40,000 employees. Although I met some good people and learned a great deal, my heart simply wasn't in it. But the idea of selling 3-D printers really excited me! Just 30 days earlier I made up my mind that I was going to sell this technology—and now I was holding the proverbial "tiger by the tail." But, sitting at my desk and reading technical data about my new product line, I felt overwhelmed. As I tried to decipher the engineering jargon, I remember saying to myself, "Chris, this is exactly the job you wanted—you will figure it out!" Eager to start, I decided to take the initiative. It was at that moment that I opened my notebook and wrote down my one-year plan for success.

The first thing I did was take an inventory of my assets. I had a company laptop, a phone, and a 3-D printing demo room. I also had access to a full-time applications engineer as well as an extensive contact database with thousands of prospects I could call. Final analysis? I had been given all of the tools I needed to succeed, ranging from technology to resources. These tools eliminated any legitimate excuse for failure on my part. Although my territory and the industry were highly competitive, I wasn't worried. Working hard and taking ownership would be my strategy! My first year, I arrived to work early, stayed late, and ate lunch in my cubicle. I saved all of my studying for after hours, to avoid dipping into my productivity while at work. Each evening after dinner, I watched industry-related YouTube videos on my laptop. Anytime I was in my vehicle or at the gym I listened to audiobooks on how to sell— Zig Ziglar was definitely my favorite!

My one-year game plan was broken down into three categories: 1) Get the Tools, 2) Do the Work, 3) Hit the Mark. *Get the Tools* pertained to all of the product knowledge and sales training I would have to acquire. To achieve my goals, my first 12 months would be like drinking from a fire hose! *Do the Work* related to being the first one to arrive at the office and the last one to leave—at least until I became a profitable asset for my employer. *Hit the Mark* was all about performance. Like the saying goes: If you don't get the purchase order, you're just a professional visitor. My efforts would be futile unless I could monetize them. There's a fine line between activity and productivity—the difference is revenue.

Today, just four years later, I'm enjoying a successful and fulfilling career while selling the same product line. As of now, I am currently ranked in the top one percent of sales reps in my industry—worldwide. I share this detail to help highlight the importance of taking ownership and doing the work. In my opinion, sales and negotiations are amongst the most challenging and rewarding careers available. If you work for a good company, sell a product you believe in, put in the effort, and take care of your customers, there is no limit to what you can achieve. So get the tools, do the work, and hit the mark!

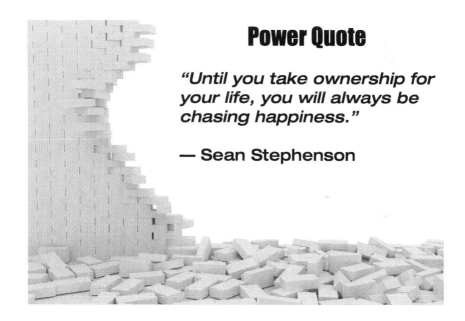

Power Quote

"Until you take ownership for your life, you will always be chasing happiness."

— Sean Stephenson